CW00664051

SEMINOLE PATCHWORK
with GLENDA FROST

LOTHIAN AUSTRALIAN *Craft* SERIES

SEMINOLE PATCHWORK
with GLENDA FROST

A Lothian Book

To Mum and Dad

A Lothian book

Lothian Publishing Company Pty Ltd
A division of Thomas C. Lothian Pty Ltd
11 Munro Street, Port Melbourne, Victoria 3207

First published 1993

Copyright © Glenda Frost 1993

All rights reserved. No part of this publication may be
reproduced, stored in a retrieval system or transmitted in
any form by any process without the prior permission of
the copyright owner. Enquiries should be made to the
publisher.

National Library of Australia
Cataloguing-in-Publication data:

Frost, Glenda, 1938– .
    Seminole patchwork with Glenda Frost.

    Includes index.
    ISBN 0 85091 583 X.

    1. Patchwork – Patterns. 2. Seminole Indians – Costume
and adornment. I. Title. (Series: Lothian Australian craft
series).

746.46041

Cover and text design by Zoë Murphy
Photography by Simon Peter Fox Photography
Illustrations by Rohan Frost

Typeset in Garth by Butler Graphics Pty Ltd
Printed in Australia by Impact Printing

Note
All garments and projects in this book were designed and made
by Glenda Frost.

Acknowledgements

My sincere thanks to Maggie Camfield, writer and freelance
editor, for her encouragement and help in writing this book
and making my dream a reality. Loving gratitude to many
helpers – my son Rohan Frost, electrical draughtsman, for his
patient support and wonderful graphic illustrations; to Simon
Peter Fox, teacher and photographer, for his photographs; to
those special people, my models: Georgina Peters, Roseanne
D'Silva, Tanya D'Silva, Sarah Frost, Amelia Seeber, Leah Baker
and Melanie Baker. Thanks too to Vicki Attoe for lending
'Maharani' (pictured on the back cover) and to friends and
family for extra support and help in many ways, such as
supplying props and furnishings for the photographs. Thanks
also to Montsalvat, Eltham, for providing the background for
some of the photographs; and to my mother, my brother Barry
and my daughter Debbie for their much-needed support and
help with paperwork.

Contents

This black velvet gown is trimmed with Seminole patchwork and embellished with jewels. It won a Special Merit trophy in Australian Gown of the Year, 1990.

Introduction

While teaching traditional American and English patchwork and quilting on Philip Island about twelve years ago I was looking for new ideas and techniques and discovered the American Indian craft of Seminole patchwork. As a result, I have spent the last nine years extending this simple, quick-to-learn, intriguing form of art.

I found that in this kind of patchwork I could use colour and texture like a brush and palette, then by embellishing with satin braids, sequins and jewels, could add a whole new dimension to the craft. I have been using this to enhance my clothing designs ever since and in 1988 introduced my version of Seminole patchwork into lavish haute couture gowns, with exciting results.

I have also adapted the traditional Italian technique of trapunto to create the same effect in an easier way. I use a bodkin threaded with acrylic macrame cord to fill the channelling, and the trapunto look gives a sophisticated finish to any garment or project.

Recently I extended my range of projects into home decorations such as the dramatic 'leadlight' blind which you will find in this book.

Seminole patchwork is easy to learn and gives you stunning results very quickly. You can add to the simple designs in this book in infinite ways to enhance your creativity and enjoyment of this wonderful craft.

Glenda Frost

Part One:
About the Craft of Seminole

Traditional Seminole Patchwork

Originally known as the Creek Nation and living in the area that is now Alabama and Georgia, the Seminole Indians were gradually pushed out of their lands by settlers during the 18th century.

They eventually settled in Florida, then owned by the Spanish, and became successful farmers, owning large herds of horses and cattle.

The Seminoles — a word that probably meant undomesticated — gave refuge to run-away slaves from the American cotton plantations, and were hated by the Southerners. The American government bought Florida from Spain in 1819. Seminole farms and villages were attacked when the Indians refused to hand over the black escapees, and fighting between the Creeks and the American military did not cease until 1842.

Several hundred Seminoles took refuge in the tropical Everglades, where their unique form of patchwork is thought to have developed. The South has long been a leading cotton producer, and the original buckskin of the Creeks in Alabama was replaced by cotton, which was better suited to the climate of the Florida Everglades and readily available.

In 1896 a railroad to Miami was opened and the Seminole Indians were able to sell their craft work to tourists. With the cash they earned they bought treadle sewing machines. When the first store was opened in Miami it was stocked with bright cotton cloth for the Indians to buy.

Traditionally they had decorated their plain cottons with hand-pieced patchwork to brighten it up. This slow hand work rapidly gave way to a new style of patchwork they designed to be made more quickly by sewing machine. By the 1920s they were using horizontal bands of patchwork and beginning to experiment with intricate designs.

Between 1935 and 1940 many new smaller and more complex patterns were invented. Since the 1940s tourism has meant that Seminole women have sewn garments for sale rather than use by their families.

While patterned materials were used by the Seminoles in the 1920s, they generally used plain brightly coloured fabrics by the 1930s, the period seen as the highpoint of the traditional form of this craft.

The Seminole Patchwork Technique

The basic principle of this craft is to sew together strips of different materials, then cut across the strips and sew the pieces together, arranged in various patterns. The resulting pieces of patchwork are then sewn into a garment of one colour, around the bottom of a skirt or shirt, for example. The offset pieces of material set up contrasting and complementary colours and patterns which catch and hold the eye. The Seminole Indians used rickrack braid to embellish their patchwork, but I like to highlight and add detail and texture by sewing ribbons and braids along the strips of colour and by adding embellished bars.

Choice of Materials

Poplin, polycotton, broderie, lawn and chintz are suitable materials for your first efforts at Seminole patchwork, but as you master the technique you may wish to turn your hand to silks and other more expensive materials. Materials with a clearly identifiable grain are best.

There is no reason why printed fabric cannot be used as well as solid colours. If chosen carefully, it can give more life to a band of patchwork. But be selective because busy patterns can detract from the contrast between colours that is a highlight of Seminole patchwork.

Colour Hints

• When cutting your fabrics, you can cut your favourite colours wider.

• A dark background will make the colours stand out vibrantly. If black is used, the strips and over-locking can also be sewn in black.

• White can also be used effectively as a back-ground colour with subtle off-whites or pastels for the patchwork.

• If you are making a garment that will be worn at night you will need to balance the colours in night light as well as in daylight. Some colours, such as purple, mauve and magenta, seem to fade out, dull off or lose their colour under artificial lighting.

• To create a vibrant look with a particular colour, use it in two or three different shades. When embellishing, choose ribbons and braids in the same shades.

• Gold braids give an antique finish while pearly braids or ribbons give a lustrous ivory or milk–opal effect.

Equipment
'Salem' ruler, cutting wheel and cutting board

Equipment

(Asterisked items are more expensive and not essential for beginners, though they will save time.)

• Tape measure

• Scissors

• Fabrics of your choice

• Cottons

• Acrylic macrame cord*

• Trimmings such as macrame beads, feathers, ribbons, braids and lace

• Marking pencil or dressmaker's chalk

• Sewing machine

• Pins

• Bodkin (a special needle used for cording)

• Rouleau hook (for turning a rouleau cord right side out)

• 'Olpha' or 'Kai' cutter*– these are brand names of a cutter consisting of a circular blade on a wheel and shaft. Polyester and other synthetic materials tend to blunt these cutters, but you can buy extra blades.

• 'Salem' or other wide, clear-plastic ruler*.

• Cutting board*. This is an expensive item but it is essential if you are going to use a Salem ruler and cutter.

• Overlocker*. Many sewing machines have an overlocking function which you can use to prevent fraying. Alternatively you can seal raw edges with a row of zigzag.

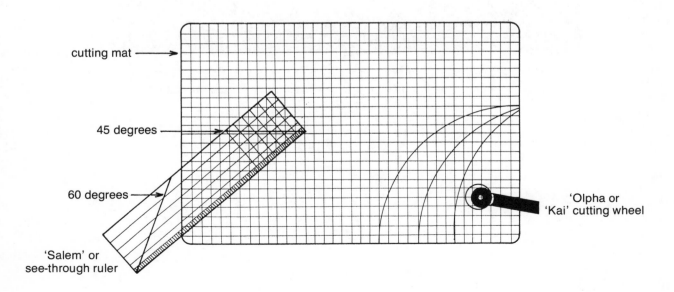

cutting mat

45 degrees

60 degrees

'Salem' or see-through ruler

'Olpha or 'Kai' cutting wheel

In this wedding coat Seminole patchwork is used with different shades of cream to create subtle textures with a variety of fabrics, braids and pearls.

Part Two:
How To Do Seminole Patchwork

Basic Techniques

Marking and Cutting Strips

Traditionally the strips of material for Seminole patchwork were cut to follow the lengthwise grain of the fabric, parallel to the selvedges, to minimise stretch, but if pieces are cut across the grain from selvedge to selvedge or on shorter pieces, they will work successfully. If your material is shorter than it is wide, strips can be cut crosswise to maximise length.

Basically you need to be able to cut straight parallel lines, first along the length of the materials and then across the width of the finished stripping (see illustration on page 12).

Sewing lines must be kept straight and parallel. If the stripping is uneven the pieces will not allow an even flow of colour and the overall effect will be lost. The patchwork will also be very difficult to put together!

As a beginner you may not want to pay for a cutting board and cutter. The alternative is to measure and rule carefully. Use a marker or wash-off pencil that shows clearly on your fabric. Measure the width of the strip carefully in several places, mark it with a visible dot and then join the dots to form a straight line. Then cut the material with scissors.

As you become more confident you may want to use the cutting wheel and board. If so, fold the material into two layers before cutting. Pin two layers of fabric together and cut through both layers at the same time. Pressure on your Salem ruler and cutter will prevent the fabric from moving when used on a cutting board.

As the cutter is very sharp, cut across in front of your body from left to right if you are right handed. Leaning in will give you more pressure. You will have good control if you put pressure on the see-through ruler with the left hand and use the 'Olpha' cutter with the right hand.

Stripping and Sewing Your Strips Together

1 Cut strips of fabric to the width you want, allowing 6 mm on each side for seams. The narrowest strip could be about 25 mm wide, which would give you a strip of 13 mm when sewn. The widest could be 8–10 cm. Remember to cut wider strips in the fabric of the colour you wish to be dominant.

2 Arrange the strips to check colours. At the start, it is best to have only five to eight colour strips. The outside strips are your main or background colour – the colour of the skirt, jacket, or whatever you are making. If you have the basic overall colour on the edges, it will blend the patchwork into the garment, rather than looking as if it has been added on top.

3 When stripping (sewing the strips together), to make sure seams are straight and even follow the inside edge of your machine foot if it is the correct width (6 mm) from the needle and therefore the seam. If your foot is too wide and your machine does not have a measuring attachment, stick a piece of masking tape on the throat plate beside the foot. Do this accurately as strips that are not even and parallel will create problems with the next step.

4 Overlock or zigzag seam edges together to prevent fraying and to neaten. Some overlocking machines have a straight sew and overlock in one action, which saves sewing time. Otherwise use the zigzag stitch available on most machines.

The overlocking or zigzag helps to prevent fraying or unravelling, but it is not absolutely essential. The Seminole Indians did not have overlocking machines when they first worked out this method, and their garments gave long wear.

5 Don't worry about tying off cottons at the end of stripping as you'll be cutting through the sewing when you re-cut your pieces.

Stripping is the first step in making Seminole patchwork.

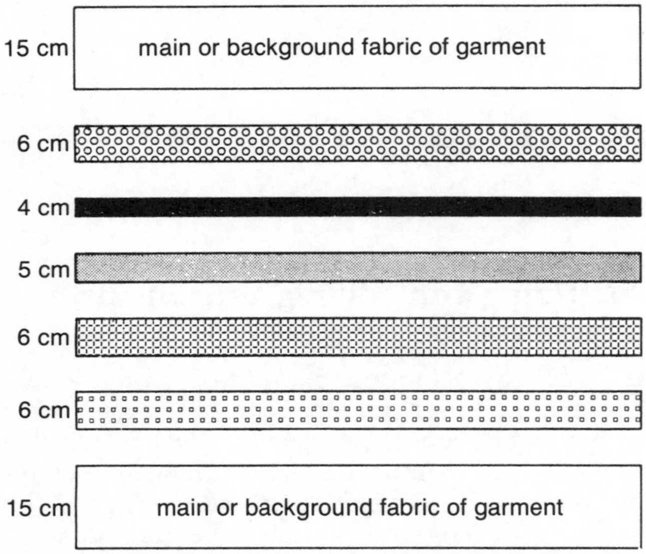

15 cm	main or background fabric of garment
6 cm	
4 cm	
5 cm	
6 cm	
6 cm	
15 cm	main or background fabric of garment

When the strips are sewn together you can add braids, ribbons or rickrack to highlight or complement the colours.

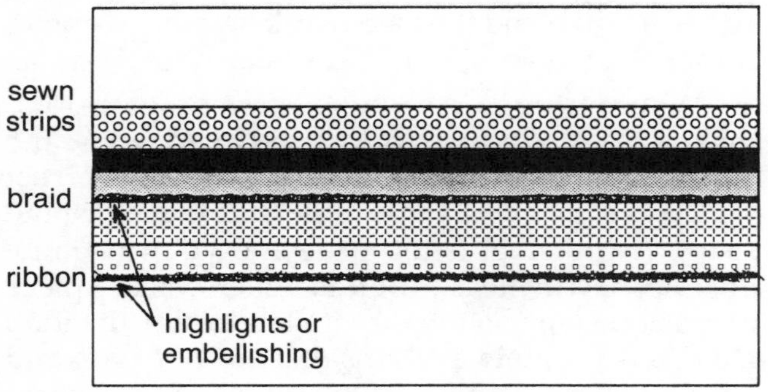

sewn strips

braid

ribbon

→ highlights or embellishing

Recutting presewn stripping into 5-cm strips for variations on scalloped design

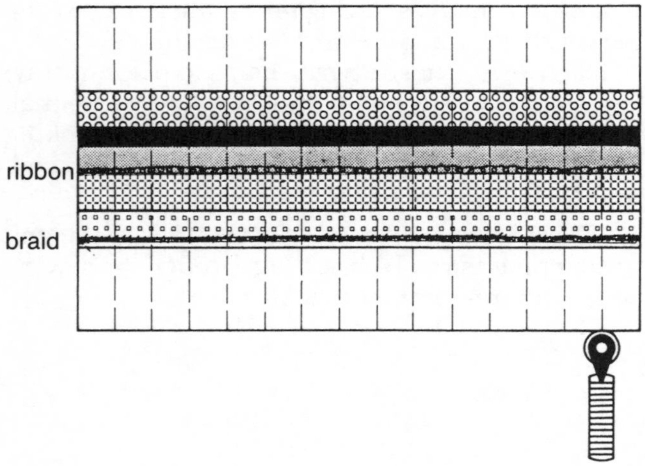

ribbon

braid

Recutting presewn stripping into 7-cm strips

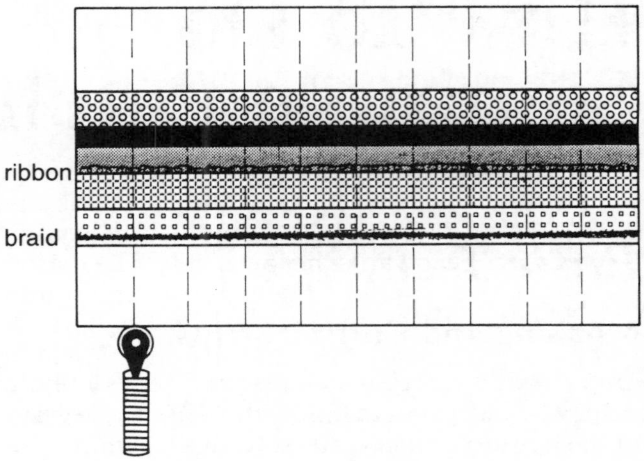

ribbon

braid

Straight joining of strips at right angles to make a set

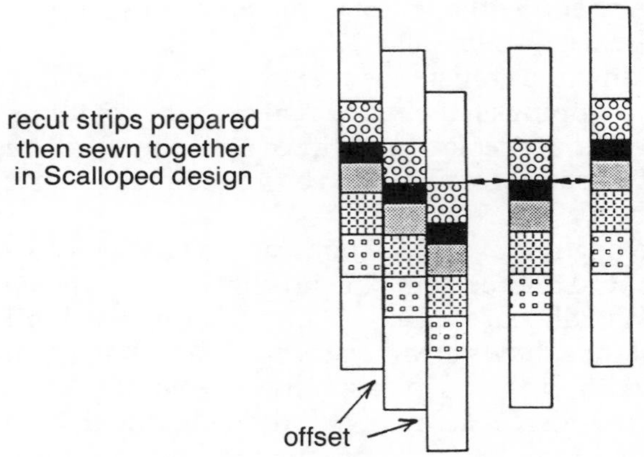

recut strips prepared then sewn together in Scalloped design

offset

Angled design

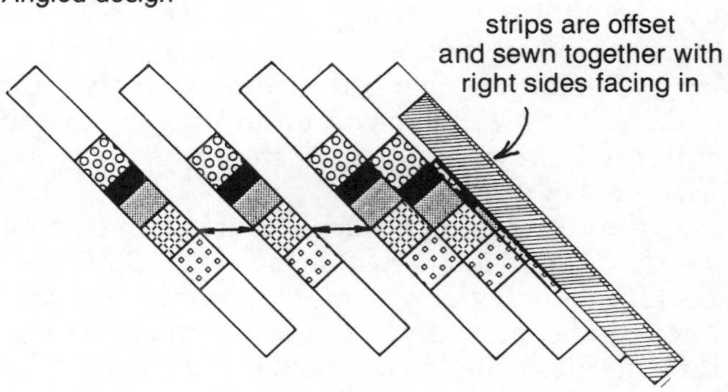

strips are offset and sewn together with right sides facing in

Ironing the stripping

Before you iron the stripping, you need to decide which way up it should go. The best way to do this is with a mirror (a reflecting window will do at a pinch). Stand about two metres away, hold up your sewn piece and look at it critically. Half closing your eyes often helps. Then decide which side looks better at the top.

Press all seams in one direction – towards the bottom or outer edge of the garment. The ironing must always be towards the lower side. The reason for this is that you will recut the stripping into pieces, arrange them then resew them to form the patchwork. Ironing in the same direction will help when sewing, as the stripping will move more smoothly under the presser foot of the machine and the finish will be neater if all seams go in one direction.

Don't overpress. Don't worry if the material 'puffs' a bit – a little puffiness increases the liveliness of the patchwork. If you press the life out of it your patchwork may end up looking like printed fabric.

Embellishing

Ribbons and braids can be used to highlight a colour. Embellishing with a complementary colour lights up the background colour and makes it glow; for example, a dull purple will come to life if highlighted with shiny purple ribbon. This effect doesn't hit you in the eye and can give greater subtlety of tone or vibrancy to some colours. A tiny dash of white will highlight and freshen the overall look, too.

If you find that you have used fabrics that don't really go together after all, embellishing can do wonders in holding the fabric colours together.

Gold and silver braids can also be used to create a jewel-like effect. Don't be afraid to dazzle – you won't go overboard and make the garment too gaudy as the basic colour will frame the bright patchwork and tone it down a little.

Embellishing must always be done before the stripping is recut to prepare it for patchwork. Snuggle the ribbon into the seam line first, then sew the opposite side down. Alternatively ribbon or braid can be sewn carefully down the centre of a fabric strip.

Don't pull braids, rickrack or ribbon towards you or pin them down while sewing. If you do you will end up with a banana curve in the fabric. When you cut across the stripping to prepare pieces of patchwork you need a straight edge.

Some of the ends of the stripping will need to be trimmed across in a straight line before you start embellishing – this will help you minimise waste in the use of ribbons and braids.

If you have a favourite or special piece of braid or ribbon which is not long enough for stripping, save it to use in the bars which separate the sets of patchwork.

Cutting the stripping

When you have sewn the strips of different materials together you have the basic stripping ready to be cut and sewn to form a band of patchwork. Cut across the strips into pieces about 5 cm wide. (The width will vary with the project – the egg cosy, for example, uses minipatchwork whereas a larger project such as a table cloth or bedspread might require strips of about 12 cm wide.) If you use 5-cm widths, the stripping visible in the finished project will be about 4 cm wide after seams are sewn.

Beginners should always cut the stripping straight, at a 90-degree angle – you can achieve a diagonal or angled effect by the way you arrange the patchwork.

Pieces can be cut diagonally to give different designs, but this is trickier and the result is often not as effective as the designs you gain from straight cutting. When a piece is cut diagonally it can be at any chosen angle, but the angle must be consistent. This method takes more time and material, but it can be an exciting experiment and may look very effective. The greater the angle the more of the background main colour will be needed so that you have sufficient when cutting the straight edges at top and bottom after pieces are sewn.

Important note:
A 'Salem' or other see-through ruler has 45-degree and 60-degree angles marked for guidance in cutting diagonal strips. To cut into 90-cm and 50-cm fabric, you fold the fabric across the width with selvedges flush together. With raw edges close to you, straighten the edges and cut through two layers. Put the 15-cm edge of the ruler across the fabric and match the 60-cm edge of the ruler along the selvedges to give you a straight line. If you want a strip 5 cm wide, simply lay your ruler across on the 5 cm mark and wheel cutter firmly across the top of the ruler, using the edge as a guide. Slide your ruler across the fabric away from you to the next 5-cm mark and repeat the procedure.

Bars

Although not used in traditional Seminole patchwork, bars can be used to make the patchwork borders or strips go further. They can be made from the main fabric colour, which can be embellished, or you can use one of the other chosen fabrics for a different effect. Embellished bars give the patchwork a luxurious finish, so it is not cheating to make your patchwork go further! Bars also break the repetition and allow for contrast and greater interest. They can make the whole patchwork look more intricate.

You need to decide how far apart to put the bars. A suggested average is every five to seven pieces, as an odd number of pieces gives a more balanced effect. This will also depend on factors such as the width of the stripping and of the cut pieces, the shape of your garment, whether you have enough patchwork to complete your garment with only a few bars and the overall effect you want.

Styles in Seminole

At last count, there seemed to be about fifty different variations within the Seminole style of patchwork, but this is only limited by the imagination. You may want to discover some further variations for yourself, but those given here, which are the three main styles, will give you plenty of scope.

Scalloped Style

The scalloped style uses stripping cut on a 90-degree angle (as illustrated below) and sewn straight. As you can see in the illustration, this style creates the effect of a wave-like movement. For this reason it is often used around the hem of a skirt. This is the simplest Seminole style, yet it is very effective. The bars set between blocks of patchwork help to set it off.

Scalloped style: the pieces are set straight but create a curving, scallop-like pattern.

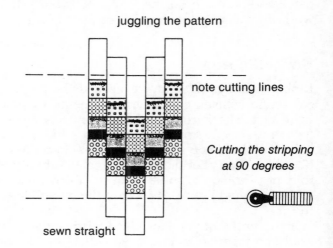

Cutting the stripping at 90 degrees

Cutting bars and embellishing

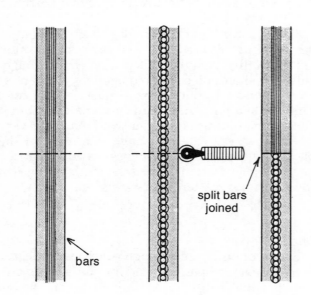

Pin your bars so that they are lined up evenly beside each set of pieces (see 'Variations Using Bars or Wider Centre Strip' on page 17).

Scalloped design with bar

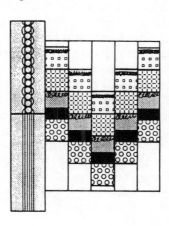

Variables in the scalloped style are the number of pieces between each bar — always an odd number for balance; the width you cut the pieces; and the height of your arrangements.

Variation is achieved in the angled style by changing the angle and the colour alignment — the wider the background strips of the basic fabric, the more contrast you can obtain with the pattern.

Scalloped design showing sets and blocks

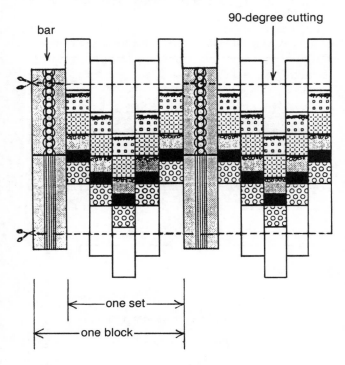

Angled style with bar trimmed

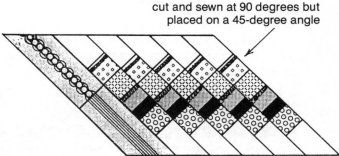

Another variation on angled style is to place half the stripping so that it runs in the opposite direction to gain a mirror-image effect (see illustration below). This design is used in the hatband and wallhanging projects (see pages 22 and 57).

Piecing to give the mirror effect which is suitable for a quilt or poncho or as a motif on the back of a jacket.

Angled Style

In this style, the strips are cut at a 90-degree angle but set at an angle of 45 degrees. With this style of patchwork you need to be very careful that your pieces are set correctly.

Angled style: setting pieces at a 45-degree angle gives greater contrast between different colours and an altogether different effect.

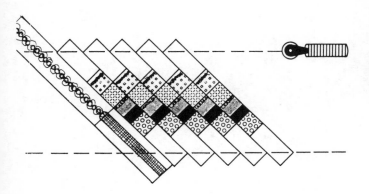

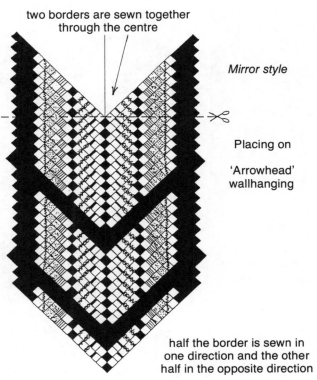

Zigzag Style

For this style the patchwork strips are cut at an angle of 45 degrees (half one way and half in the opposite direction, as shown in the illustration below), then pieced together at right angles. This changes the patchwork composition from little squares to angled diamonds and gives a quite different effect from the other two main styles.

Note:
Cutting on an angle has potential problems, so be careful to keep the angle consistent. A wide, see-through ruler with angles marked for the degree of angle you want will certainly help.

Zigzag style: the patchwork is cut on a 45-degree angle and sewn at right angles to give a zigzag effect. Bars can also be added.

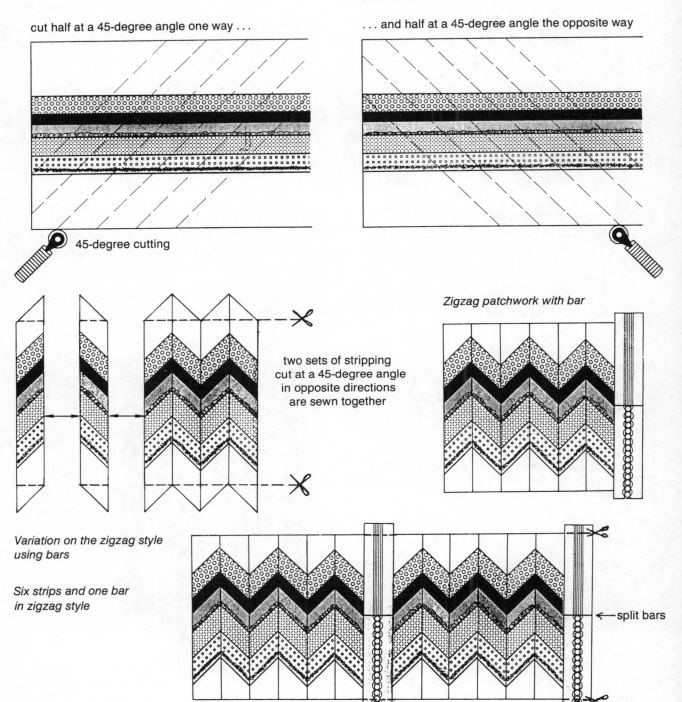

cut half at a 45-degree angle one way . . .

. . . and half at a 45-degree angle the opposite way

45-degree cutting

two sets of stripping
cut at a 45-degree angle
in opposite directions
are sewn together

Zigzag patchwork with bar

*Variation on the zigzag style
using bars*

*Six strips and one bar
in zigzag style*

←—split bars

The 'Pacific Jewel' kimono jacket (left) *is slimming and versatile — one size fits many. It can also be made as a man's shaving jacket.*

The 'Lapis Lazuli' poncho (right) *won first prize in the Limmits Craft Award in Australian Gown of the Year, 1989. The poncho is fully reversible with Seminole patchwork on one side and a handpainted and jewelled phoenix with cornelli embroidery on the other. (Photograph location courtesy Montsalvat Arts Centre, Eltham, Victoria)*

Top: 'Peaches and Cream' table accessories. *The patchwork in these matching table mats, napkin rings and tea cosy can be colour coordinated with your dining room.*
The drawstring bag is a versatile addition to your wardrobe.

Above: The 'Wedgwood' bedroom collection. *This pillow case, tray cloth, hot water bottle cover and egg cosy can be made from leftover pieces of Seminole patchwork or in matching sets.*

Variations Using Bars or Wider Centre Strip

All three styles can be varied by the use of bars, as follows.

The scalloped style can be varied by using a wider centre strip, of 7 cm, as shown below.

1 Usually bars are cut 7–10 cm wide. The length depends on the length of the finished set when it has been trimmed evenly on top and bottom.

Variations on the Scalloped style using wider centre strip

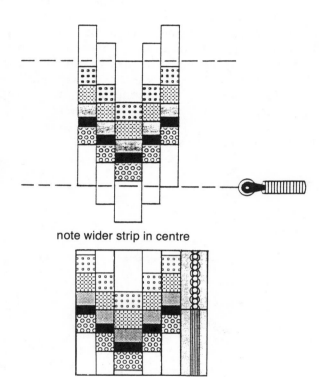

note wider strip in centre

2 Work out the number of blocks to be used for the garment or project to discover the length of fabric needed for the bars.

3 When embellishing the bars, keep the lace, ribbon or braid 13 mm in from the raw edges — otherwise they will be lost in the seam.

4 Another method is to make split bars to add yet another dimension of colour contrasts to the design of the patchwork. Prepare two different embellished bars, adding 6-mm seam allowance per join for each bar.

5 Sew embellished half bars together across the width, then overlock or zigzag seam to neaten.

Note: If you plan to set your pieces on an angle (as in the Angled style), you will need to cut bars a good 5–7.5 cm longer than the prepared set of stripping so that it lines up correctly. This is a little tricky, so be careful. The greater the angle of the pattern the longer you will need to make the bars. Practise by placing a length of bar between two finished sets of pieced patchwork.

note plain unsplit bar

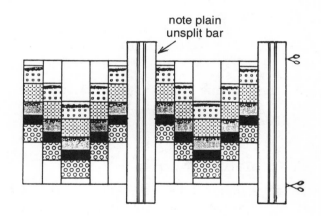

Angle-set patchwork with bar— bars must be cut longer!

note extended bars

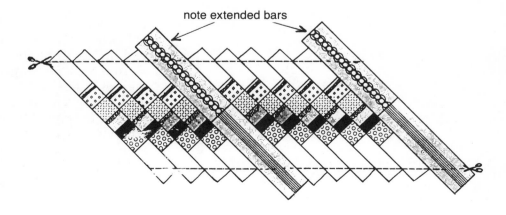

Other Variations

Other variations, and there are many, can be obtained by:

- inserting one-colour strips between the pieces
- placing pieces at different angles
- turning pieces upside down
- reverse cutting half the pieces.

After you have reverse cut half the pieces you can use the leftover triangle of stripping in the Apache bag or poncho, which can easily incorporate any colour-matched experiments you make with different styles of patchwork.

As you become more familiar with the technique, you will find that you can foresee what arrangements of colours in strips will look like when they have been cut and pieced together.

You need wider strips of the garment's basic background colour to allow for the movement of your strips of colour when you have recut and sewn them. The wider the strips of the main colour, the more you can juggle the colours. You will lose some of the main colour at both top and bottom when you cut straight across the ends of the pieces to neaten off. The Scalloped design needs the most extra material.

Keep your eye on certain spots such as ribbons, braid or strong colours so that you line the pieces up correctly. If you like you can use pins or chalk marks to help.

When sewing pieces together, make sure your seam allowance is consistent or part of the effect will be lost.

Completing the Band

When your blocks have been sewn and overlocked trim the jagged edges of your background colour so that you have a band of Seminole patchwork that is ready to be applied to the garment.

Trapunto — the Italian Art of Cording

Traditional trapunto is made by sewing the outlines of your design and then stuffing this section with a soft thread or material to give it a raised, embossed look. The Italians have been decorating their clothes with trapunto for centuries — Lucretia Borgia may have worn gowns with trapunto decoration during the Renaissance.

The traditional method is very time-consuming, however, and a similar effect can be gained simply by using a bodkin, normally used for elastic. A bodkin is a stainless steel needle with a round tip. It has a split right through the centre which staples yarn so it won't slip. It also has a large eye, so threading yarn through the eye is easy. You can pull the yarn down the split to the end, as shown in the illustrations below.

Threading the bodkin for trapunto

split

thread cord through
eye of bodkin

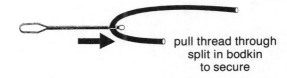
pull thread through
split in bodkin
to secure

Method

For a hem, cuffs or bands, cut material twice the width you want for the finished article plus a 12-mm seam allowance. Fold in half across width with right side out, press, then sew at 12-mm intervals. You will make three, four or five 'channels' for the cord, depending on your pattern. A 15-cm width folded in half will give you five channels and seam allowance.

Always make sure you leave about 5 cm of acrylic macrame cord spare at each end as it appears to shrink as you thread more and more channels.

1 Thread 7-ply acrylic macrame cord into the bodkin, and push this through each of the channels (see illustration below).

2 The easiest way to use the bodkin is to push it eye first through the channels. Make sure that all puckers are smoothed out as you complete each channel. The thread will fill the channel and give a traditional trapunto or corded finish.

3 When attaching trapunto to clothes, it is easier not to thread it first, but to make the channels, sew it neatly onto the garment, then thread. This gives the foot on your machine the space to make the seam line where you want it – on the last stitched channel.

Threading the trapunto channels

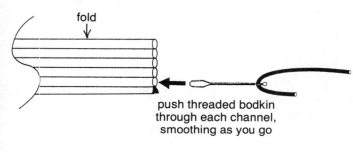

push threaded bodkin
through each channel,
smoothing as you go

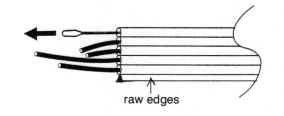

raw edges

Ideas for trapunto finishes: bands, cuffs and hems

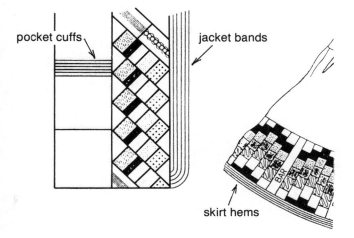

pocket cuffs

jacket bands

skirt hems

Rouleau Cords

Traditionally rouleau cords are cut on the bias, using a square piece of fabric and cutting diagonally. This gives a fine rouleau suitable for decoration.

For the projects in this book, however, all the rouleau cords are cut and sewn on the straight grain of the fabric. This is because most of the uses for rouleau here put strain on the cord and the stitching would break if the rouleau was sewn on the bias.

Materials

Rouleau hook. This is an ingenious gadget which makes the process very simple. You can also use it for threading macrame beads onto rouleau cords (see illustrations below).

A piece of fabric 25 mm wide and 90 cm long.

Method

1 Place fabric right side up and fold in half lengthwise. Sew along the fabric 6 mm in from the fold to make a channel.

2 Push the rouleau hook through the channel to the end. Make sure the hook secures well into the fabric at the end then pull it back inside the channel to turn it right side out (see illustration below).

Using a rouleau hook

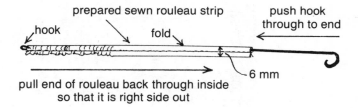

prepared sewn rouleau strip

push hook
through to end

hook

fold

6 mm

pull end of rouleau back through inside
so that it is right side out

Thread cord on hook and pull through macrame bead

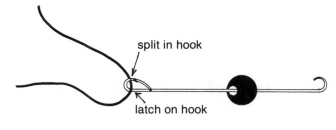

split in hook

latch on hook

The 'Wayfarer' nomad dress has several different styles of Seminole patchwork in the yolk and the angled design in the skirt border.

Part Three:
Projects in Seminole Patchwork

Rejuvenating Your Wardrobe

The aim here is to enhance existing items by adding patchwork you have made. Of course you can also make the items from scratch or, if you prefer, buy the items and personalise them with your own patchwork decoration. Pieces of patchwork used as pockets, collars or yokes can enliven plain or older clothes.

Note:
To square off the edges of patchwork neatly, use the method suggested for the kimono jacket, page 45, using a finish of braids and mitred corners.

Collars and Yokes

If you want to design your own collar or yoke, first sketch your dress, jacket or top, then draw alternative designs for a very neat and decorative look, edge your collar or yoke with ribbon or braid, as shown for the Apache top on page 52.

Shirts and Dresses

A strip or shape of patchwork can really brighten up clothes that have seen better days. Choose your colours and make enough stripping. The style of your garment will dictate the appropriate trim, but you can also use your imagination. A peasant shirt may lend itself to tassels and ribbons, an Indian/plain shirt may look wonderful with a few feathers or shells – remember, this technique was evolved by people who lived close to nature.

Patches

Patches look great if they're a design accent made from patchwork. Be sure you have an ample piece to cover not only the tear or mark, but the surrounding area as well. You can cover knees and elbows with super patches, but you don't need a tear or hole as an excuse!

Track Pants, Jeans and Other Children's Clothes

Pants can have a strip of patchwork added to give them new life. It's an easy way to lengthen the life of favourite children's clothes when they're growing.

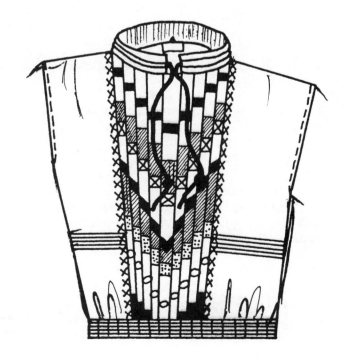

Using Add-on Patchwork

Often you will find you have a small amount of patchwork left over fter you have made a garment, wall hanging or accessory. Below are some more suggestions.

'Persian Jewel' Hatband

Materials

- Prepared patchwork 7.5 cm wide and 70 cm long
- Lining material 7.5 cm wide and 70 cm long

1 Use three pieces of prestripped, presewn, braided and embellished patchwork. Cut them 35 mm wide and sew together, using a 6-mm seam allowance. Overlock or zigzag to neaten.

2 Another three strips must be cut 35 mm wide, but they will be pieced and sewn reversed so that they seem to reflect the first three strips. This procedure will give a mirror finish (as shown on page 15).

Hatband mirror patchwork, cut at 90 degrees and placed on a 45-degree angle

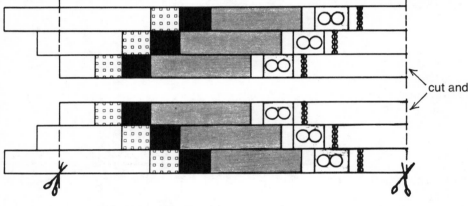

cut and join

3 Cut across the ends and trim straight. Join the two pieces of patchwork with right sides facing each other, using straight stitch and sewing on the wrong side. Press lightly.

4 Cut your piece of lining 70 cm by 7.5 cm or to the width you require. Place your patchwork piece and lining together with right sides facing.
Tack them together, leaving an opening of about 5 cm.

Finished hatband   centre join

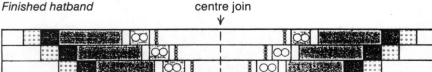

Straight stitch around all edges.
Snip corners off to eliminate bulk.
Turn through to right side and blind stitch opening.
Press.

5 If you would like to add trimming, sew cords as for the cummerbund on page 36 and add tassels, feathers or beads.

Hatband lining

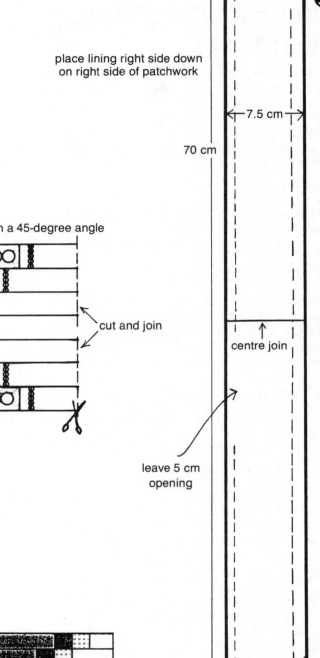

place lining right side down
on right side of patchwork

7.5 cm

70 cm

centre join

leave 5 cm
opening

'Wedgwood' Tray Cloth

Leftover Seminole patchwork can be used to brighten up an old tray cloth, or you can cut a new one to the size you want. If you like, you can sew the patchwork on to form a pocket, a handy home for napkin and utensils.

If you want to make matching napkin rings or egg cosies, buy enough material for everything. Note that while you will want matching colours and proportions of colours, the piece of patchwork for the tray cloth will be much wider and probably worked with bigger pieces than the egg cosy, for example.

Materials

- Fabric for tray cloth approximately 44 cm by 32 cm
- Patchwork piece in Scalloped style about 15 cm by 19 cm
- Pregathered lace, 2 m

Method

1 Prepare the fabric for the tray cloth by overlocking or zigzagging around all edges.

2 Zigzag or overlock all edges, then straight stitch some pregathered lace or braid across the top of the patchwork (the 15-cm edge).

3 Tack a hem of about 1 cm around the sides and bottom of the patchwork.

4 Place the patchwork evenly on the lower side of the tray cloth as shown in the illustration at right. Machine the patchwork in place with straight stitch.

Patchwork pocket for tray cloth

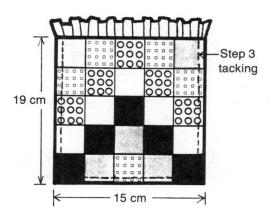

Finishing the tray cloth

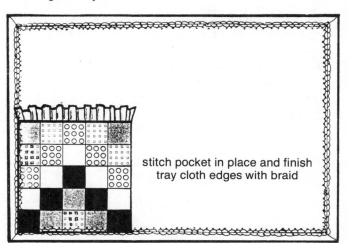

stitch pocket in place and finish tray cloth edges with braid

Cutting out for tray cloth

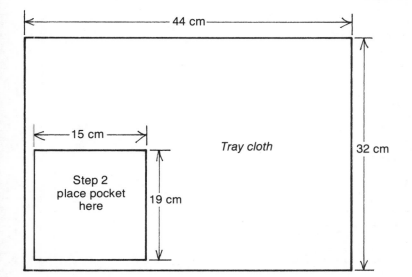

'Peaches and Cream' Place Mats

You can brighten plain table mats with patchwork or colour coordinate them with the diningroom. These instructions are for making your own mats but you can, of course, buy plain table mats to work on. If you do, begin with step 2.

Materials

- Fabric 44 cm by 32 cm for each mat (or 1 metre for six mats)
- Patchwork measuring 32 cm by 13 cm for each mat (or 2 m by 13 cm for six mats)
- Pregathered lace for edge of place mat, 1.7 m per mat
- 25-mm ribbon or braid, 32 cm per mat

Method

1 Cut fabric 44 cm by 32 cm for each mat

2 Cut a piece of patchwork 13 cm by 32 cm for each mat. Place this down one side of each place mat and tack, then straight stitch in position around all edges of the patchwork. Press.

3 Topstitch a length of braid or ribbon over the inner raw edge of the patchwork (see illustration below).

4 Overlock or zigzag around all edges of the place mat.

5 Finish all edges with braid or pregathered lace. Simply machine, straight stitch or zigzag all edges and neaten joins by handsewing.

Finished place mat

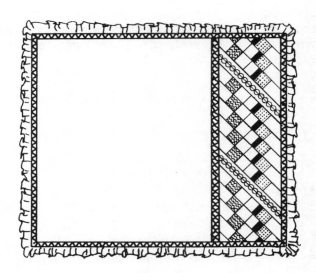

Attaching patchwork to the place mat

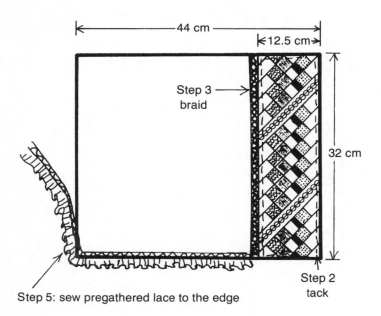

Step 3 braid

44 cm

12.5 cm

32 cm

Step 2 tack

Step 5: sew pregathered lace to the edge

'Peaches and Cream' Napkin Rings

Materials
For each napkin ring you will need:
- Patchwork, 17 cm long and 7 cm wide
- Lining, 17 cm long and 7 cm wide
- Velcro, 5 cm

Method
1 Place the lining and patchwork together with right sides facing in. Starting about 7 cm from the end, sew around all edges of the napkin ring, using a 6-mm seam allowance, as shown below. Leave a 5-cm opening.

Finished napkin ring

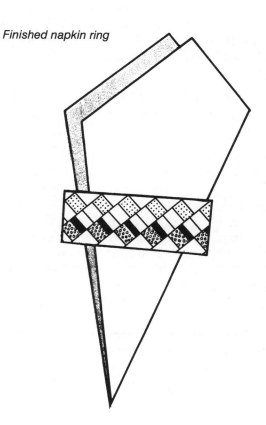

Cutting out for napkin ring

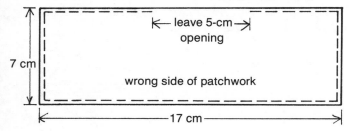

lining underneath

2 Turn the piece through the opening so that it is right side out and handsew the opening neatly.

3 Machine the fluffy side of the Velcro to the lining at one end of the napkin ring and sew the opposite piece of Velcro to the patchwork side at the other end.

How to make the napkin ring

Steps 2 & 3

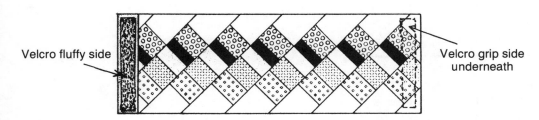

Velcro fluffy side

Velcro grip side underneath

'Wedgwood' Pillowcase

With ready-made pillowcases you will need to unpick the side seams back to the width of the patchwork piece. When the patchwork is in place restitch the pillowcase along the original seams and you will have a décor pillowcase!

Materials

For each bought or made pillowcase you will need:

- Patchwork, 51 cm long (width is optional)
- Lace, 51 cm long

Method

1 Unpick the pillowcase along the seams at the open end.

2 Place the pillowcase right side up and put the patchwork right side down along the fold of the pillowcase flap, making sure there is sufficient patchwork at each end for upper and lower seam allowances. First tack it in place, then straight stitch carefully.

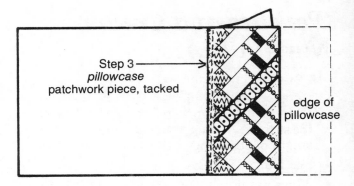

Step 3
pillowcase
patchwork piece, tacked

edge of pillowcase

4 Stitch over this overlocked edge with ribbon, lace or both, so that the edge is concealed by trim and the patchwork is attached to the pillowcase on both sides.

5 Turning the pillowcase inside out, put the unpicked flap back in place and resew the seams, catching the patchwork in along the side seams. Overlock or zigzag to finish.

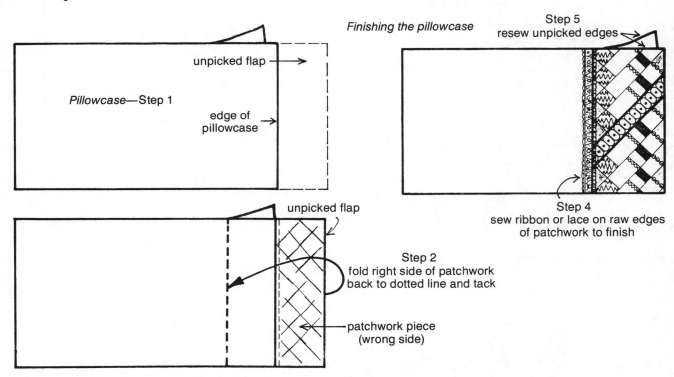

Pillowcase—Step 1

unpicked flap

edge of pillowcase

unpicked flap

Step 2
fold right side of patchwork back to dotted line and tack

patchwork piece (wrong side)

Finishing the pillowcase

Step 5
resew unpicked edges

Step 4
sew ribbon or lace on raw edges of patchwork to finish

3 Fold back so that the right side of the patchwork shows and press. There will now be a length of patchwork with a raw edge towards the centre of the pillowcase.

Zigzag or overlock that edge, then tack down.

Sew into position with 6-mm seams, sewing patchwork sides into the seams of the pillowcase.

'Maharani' Shawl

Cutting out for shawl with fabrics of different sizes

Materials

- Main shawl fabric, 1.5 m of 150-cm material or 2 m of 90-cm material
- Patchwork stripping, 90 cm long and 30 cm wide. (This is a workable size, but the width of the stripping is up to you. Basically you need one length of stripping with five or six colours.)
- Silk fringe, 3 m
- 25-mm braid, 2m

Method

1 If you have 150-cm fabric, cut the square of fabric diagonally to give enough for two shawls or for a shawl and matching bag. If you find that the shawl is too long for you, trim 5 cm off the shoulder edge. If you have 90-cm fabric, cut to the measurements shown at right.

2 Press a light fold through the centre of the shawl to the bottom point, as in the illustration below. This is a guideline for placing the patchwork.

3 Position and tack your piece of patchwork down the centre of the shawl.

4 Place the ribbon or braid to cover the raw edges of the patchwork panel and sew down on both sides. Trim off excess patchwork from wrong side of shawls.

5 Zigzag or overlock the three raw edges of the shawl to neaten it.

6 Turn a small hem of about 10 mm in on the top shoulder edge of the shawl and straight sew.

7 Fold the ends of the silk fringe under for about 5 cm at each end of the shawl to neaten. The silk fringe must then be applied to the two shorter or 'bottom' edges of the shawl to finish off. Stitch from front points of the shawl towards the bottom point, then to the opposite front point to complete.

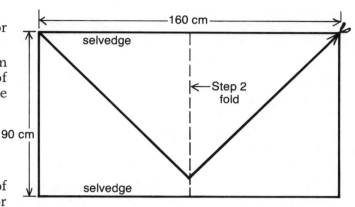

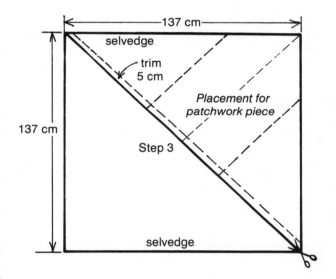

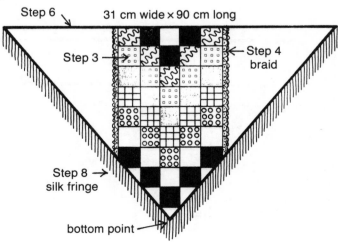

Finished shawl

'Persian Jewel' Bookmark

Materials
- Leftover piece of patchwork stripping 33 cm long and 4 cm wide.
- Lining material cut to the same size.

Method

1 Prepare as for Scalloped style (see page 14), using three presewn, braided and embellished patchwork strips 2.5 cm wide. Sew them together with 6-mm seams.

2 Cut a piece of fabric for the lining and place it against the patchwork with right sides facing. Tack them together, then straight stitch around all edges, leaving a 4-cm gap on one of the long sides.

3 Snip the corners carefully, as shown in the illustration below. This will eliminate bulky corners. Make sure you do not cut the stitching.

4 Turn the piece right side out through the gap, press, then hand sew the opening with blindstitch.

5 To obtain a V shape at the bottom, turn back the two bottom corners and handsew them together about 20 mm up from the bottom, as shown below.

You can sew a tassel to the point of the bookmark, if you like, or sew seed beads around the edges and on the patchwork.

Finished bookmark

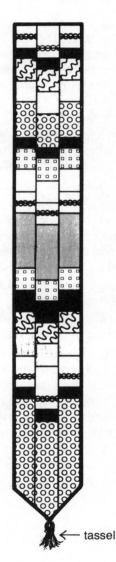

← tassel

How to make the bookmark

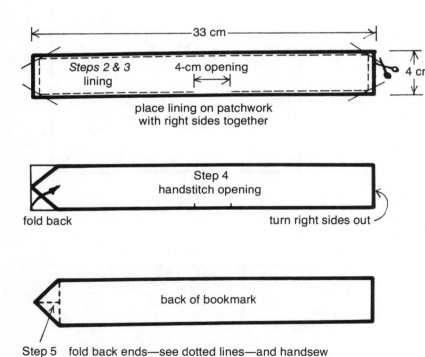

Steps 2 & 3 lining — 4-cm opening — 33 cm — 4 cm

place lining on patchwork with right sides together

Step 4 handstitch opening

fold back   turn right sides out

back of bookmark

Step 5   fold back ends—see dotted lines—and handsew

'Wedgwood' Hotwater Bottle Cover

A hotwater bottle can be made to colour coordinate with or match your bedlinen.

Materials

- A piece of patchwork 25 cm by 15 cm will suit a normal-sized hotwater bottle cover. Prepare patchwork in the angled style shown on page 15 or use leftover patchwork.
- Two pieces of cotton, poplin or chintz, 36 cm long and 25 cm wide.
- Ribbon, braid or lace, 90 cm
- Pregathered lace, 1.5 m
- Velcro, 9 cm

Method

1 With the two pieces of fabric for the back and front, measure 65 mm from centre to left and right and mark with dressmaker's chalk or pencil. This 13 cm on each side will give you a diameter of 26 cm for the neck opening.

2 Mark 12 mm down from the left and right corners of the top on both layers of fabric. Draw a line from the marks you made in Step 1 to these new marks and cut these corners off. This will give your cover a nice fit.

Cutting out for hotwater bottle cover

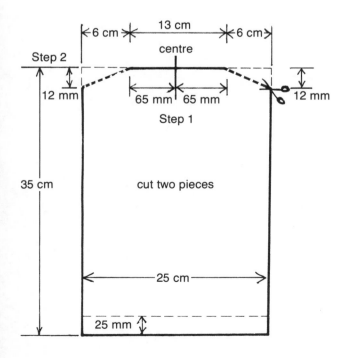

3 Overlock or zigzag all outer edges of the patchwork piece, then place it in position on the right side of one of the pieces of fabric.
Pin around all patchwork edges.
This will be the front of the cover.

4 Now you are ready to straight stitch the patchwork on to the front of the cover. To conceal the edges, embellish it with braid, ribbons or lace.

How to make the front of the hotwater bottle cover

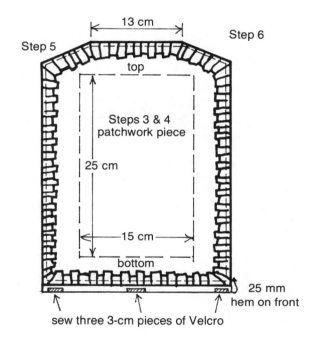

5 As there is lace inserted in the join, this must be attached to the front of the cover before the front and back are joined together.
Place the length of pregathered lace on the right side of the front cover 12 mm in from the edge.
Start at the left of the 13-cm neck opening and place the lace so that the fancy edge faces in towards the centre of the cover. Sew into position. On the bottom of the front allow 25 mm for the hem to turn under.
When you return to the neck, continue sewing so that the lace is double over this 13-cm section. This will give it a nice lush finish.

6 Fold and handsew, finishing ends of the lace back neatly.

7 To prepare the back panel of the hotwater bottle cover: with right side facing, sew two layers of pregathered lace to the edge of the top opening. Prepare the bottom opening by overlocking the edges.

8 Placing back and front panels together with right sides facing, tack edges from the bottom opening to the neck opening. Use a 13-mm seam allowance and be careful not to catch the edges of the lace into the seam.
Sew edges and overlock or zigzag to finish.

The finishing touches to the back neck

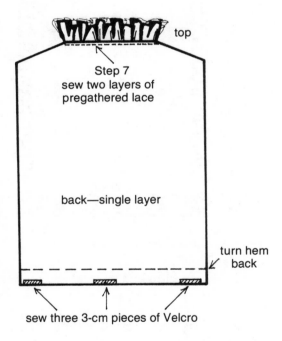

top

Step 7
sew two layers of
pregathered lace

back—single layer

turn hem
back

sew three 3-cm pieces of Velcro

Finished hotwater bottle cover

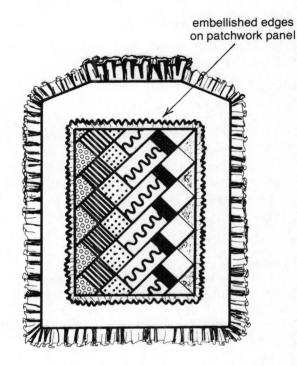

embellished edges
on patchwork panel

9 Turn a 25-mm hem on front of cover under so that it will be inside the cover. Measure across the bottom opening and pin at three equal points (see illustration above). Sew 3-cm pieces of Velcro on the bottom opening for fasteners. This will give a strong finish.

'Peaches and Cream' Dilly Bag

This simple bag design has been used for centuries. You can make it to match a skirt, poncho or jacket, using the same patchwork design or simply the same colours. The bag is unlined, so it can look dainty, especially if you use sheer fabrics such as Swiss cotton or cotton lace in the patchwork.

Materials

- Fringe or bead trim, 65 cm
- Piece of diagonal patchwork (worked in the angled design shown on page 15), 65 cm long and 25 cm wide
- Cotton, poplin or chintz fabric for bases, hem and rouleau cord, 90 cm long and 50 cm wide
- Stiff Vilene, 23 cm

Method

1   The easiest way to get a perfectly circular base is to find a dinner plate of the right size and draw around it with dressmaker's chalk. The instructions are for a bag of 20-cm diameter. The angle-design patchwork eases in well because it is sewn on the bias.

Using your plate, cut two circles of lining material and one of Vilene. Place the Vilene circle between the two lining circles, which have right sides facing out. Sew the three circles together, using a 6-mm seam allowance, to form the base of the bag.

Cutting out for dilly bag

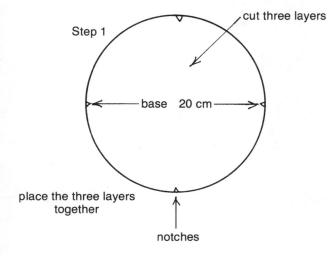

2   Sew the ends of the patchwork together to form a tube of the same circumference as the sewn circles. Zigzag or overlock to neaten (see illustration below).

The patchwork tube

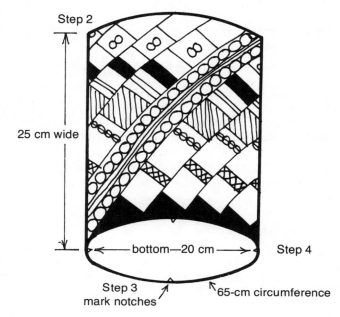

3   Fold patchwork in half from raw seam, then in quarters, and mark notches on the quarter folds. Fold the base in half then quarters and mark notches on the quarter folds.

4   Turn the tube of patchwork inside out.
Match the notches to the notches on the base and pin in place.
Straight stitch allowing 9-mm seams so that the sewing line on the base will be hidden.
Zigzag or overlock to neaten.

5   Now cut the top panel of the bag 50 cm long and 16 cm wide (this includes 13-mm hems).
Overlock or zigzag to neaten ends, then turn back the 13-mm hems.
Fold in half lengthwise, press, then straight sew 25 mm in from fold.
Straight stitch a 13-mm channel from the last row stitched, 4 cm in from the fold, for the rouleau cord to go through.
Stitch 10 mm in from raw edges.
Using this stitch line as a guide, pin and stitch the hem around the top of the bag.
Zigzag or overlock to neaten.

Top of dilly bag

Step 5

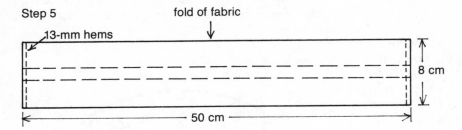

6 Make a rouleau cord as shown on page 19. It should be approximately 1 m long. Thread the cord through the channels you made at the top of the bag.
Knot the ends neatly. If you wish, thread macrame beads onto ends to finish and knot to secure the beads.

Making the rouleau cords

Step 6

7 Handstitch the beaded edge or fringe around the bottom of the bag on the edge of the patchwork, neatening off joins.

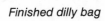

Finished dilly bag

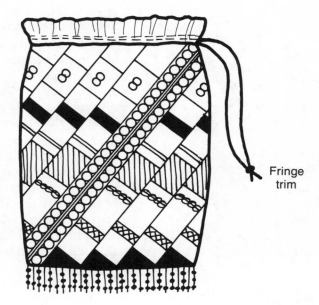

'Denim and Lace' girls' skirts *allow for the growing years with elasticised waistbands and 2-cm tucks which can be let down when needed. You can rejuvenate or lengthen an old skirt or dress with patchwork too.*

'Mischief' tabard jacket. *This lined three-quarter-length sleeveless jacket was a leisure-wear finalist in the 1991 Australian Gown of the Year. One size fits all.*

'Fireglow' skirt and cummerbund. *You can see the essence of the
Seminole craft in this elaborate splash of colour and feather trim,
wearable in all seasons. Glenda Frost's students are able to make
skirts and cummerbunds like this in a three-day workshop.
(Photograph location courtesy of Montsalvat Arts Centre,
Eltham, Victoria)*

'Monastique' (left) and 'Melba's Black Opal' (right). *Add extra length to the skirt (directions on pages 40–42) to create a glamorous evening skirt like these. 'Monastique' won first prize in 1988 at the Australian Bicentennial Quilting Symposium at Armidale, NSW, and 'Melba's Black Opal' was a finalist in the fantasy section of Australian Gown of the Year, 1988. (Photograph location courtesy of Montsalvat Arts Centre, Eltham, Victoria)*

Mini Patchwork

The size of patchwork can vary from large widths of material used for pieces such as tablecloths or quilts to tiny widths, as in this egg cosy.

'Wedgwood' Egg Cosy

Because they are so small, egg cosies will look best if you make them with patchwork made from thin strips. If you want them to match a tray cloth, place mats or napkin rings, use the same basic fabric and the same colours in your patchwork, but make the patchwork mini-sized to reflect the daintiness of an egg cosy.

Materials

For each egg cosy:

- Minipatchwork piece, 19 cm long and 9.5 cm wide
- Lining fabric of the same size
- Ribbons, braids or laces to embellish, a small amount—use scraps

Method

1 To make the piece of mini stripping, take 30-cm long strips of material and cut three strips of different colours about 25 mm wide and two outside strips 4 cm wide.
Sew the strips using 6-mm seams and overlock edges. As with all of this style of patchwork, press all seams one way, then embellish with fine ribbons and lace.

2 Make a piece of patchwork measuring 19 cm by 9.5 cm in either style (scalloped or angled) and cut pieces of stripping 25 mm wide using 6-mm seams.

3 Fold patchwork in half with right sides together and straight sew along the two sides, using a 6-mm seam allowance.

To round the top of the egg cosy, measure 25 mm down and 25 mm across from the corner of the fold and, stitch securely, following the line between these two points and allowing 6-mm seams. Backstitch at ends to hold, then cut across the corners of both sides on top of the cosy.

4 Repeat the procedures in Step 3 for the lining.

5 Turn the patchwork piece right side out, press, then push the lining into the patchwork piece so that it fits snugly.
Overlock or zigzag the bottom edges of the cosy.

The egg cosy looks pretty if you finish it off with pregathered lace stitched over the zigzag edges. The raw ends of the lace should be handstitched to neaten. A little bow can be added to the top of the egg cosy.

Finished egg cosy

Cutting out for egg cosy

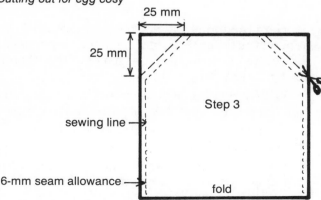

Step 3
sewing line →
6-mm seam allowance →
fold
25 mm
25 mm

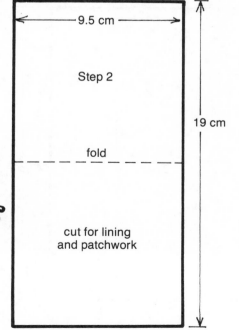

9.5 cm
Step 2
fold
19 cm
cut for lining and patchwork

Clothes and Accessories

Seminole patchwork has been used primarily as a decorative trim, although it is thought that the Seminole Indians also used it as a way of lengthening garments so that they could be worn for extended periods by growing children.

Drawstring Apache Bag

This go-anywhere bag can complement a patchwork skirt or jacket (see colour pages).

Materials
- Cotton or chintz, 90 cm long and 50 cm wide
- Small piece of patchwork about 15 cm wide by 40 cm long
- Silk fringe, 35 cm
- 25-mm braid or ribbon, 1.2 m
- Four macrame beads
- Rouleau hook for cord

Method
1 To make the back and front of the bag, cut two pieces of fabric 40 cm by 33 cm.
Cut off corners 7 cm from the bottom and sides as shown in the illustration below.

Cutting out for Apache bag

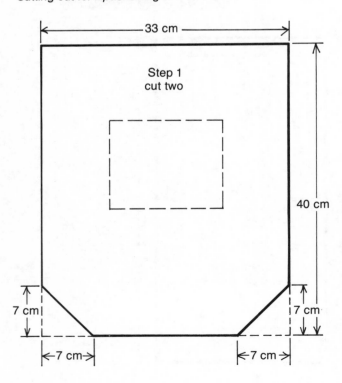

2 Cut two pieces of fabric 33 cm long and 10 cm wide for the band.

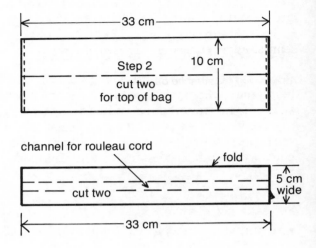

3 Cut two pieces of main fabric 1.2 m long and 5 cm wide for the rouleau cords (see page 19).

Important note:
Rouleau cords are cut on the straight grain to prevent breaking stitches if the bag is used frequently or the cords are pulled roughly.

4 To make an inside pocket for the bag, cut one piece of main fabric 15 cm by 12 cm.

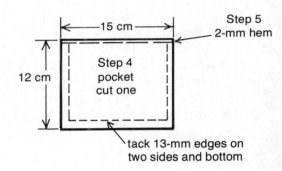

5 Hem the top of the pocket then tack a 13-mm hem on the other three sides. Place this pocket on the centre of the inside front panel of the bag and straight stitch into position.

6 With the right side of the front panel facing you, tack the piece of patchwork through the centre.

7 Straight stitch braid or ribbon over the edges of the patchwork to conceal its raw edges.

8 Sew the silk fringe upside down. It is sewn to the front of the bag 13 mm in from the bottom edge. of the bag 13 mm in from the bottom edge.

9 Place front and back of bag together with right sides facing. Sew around the side and bottom edges with a 13-mm seam allowance, making sure that you sew on the fringe stitch lines at the bottom edge.

Be careful you don't stitch the fringe to the side seams. Overlock or zigzag to neaten.

Assembling the Apache bag

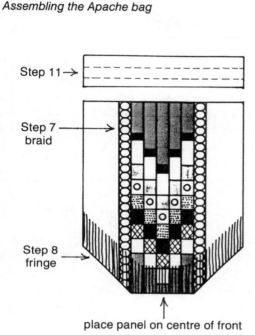

Step 11 →

Step 7 braid

Step 8 fringe

place panel on centre of front

13 Thread drawstrings through the channels on top of the bag. To do this, thread one cord through one side then around through the other side. Repeat in the opposite direction with the other drawstring, as shown in the illustration below.

Tie a knot in the drawstrings and thread with four macrame beads on each end of the cord.

Threading the drawstrings

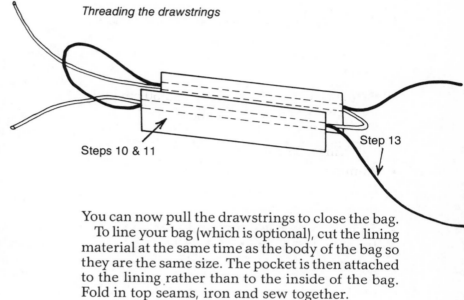

Steps 10 & 11

Step 13

You can now pull the drawstrings to close the bag.

To line your bag (which is optional), cut the lining material at the same time as the body of the bag so they are the same size. The pocket is then attached to the lining rather than to the inside of the bag. Fold in top seams, iron and sew together.

Finished Apache bag

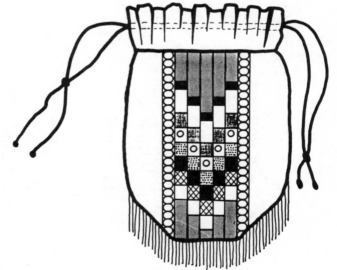

10 Take the two pieces you have cut for the top bands.

Hem the ends then fold in half lengthwise and press. Stitch one channel lengthwise 13 mm down from the fold, then another channel 30 mm down from the fold. This leaves a channel for the cord to be drawn through.

11 The two top band pieces must now be sewn to the front and back top edges of the bag.

Place the band right side inwards and sew across edges with a 6-mm seam allowance.

The top edges should fit snugly if side seam allowances have been followed.

After sewing the seams, overlock or zigzag to neaten.

12 Take the two long pieces you have cut for cords and fold them in half. With right sides inside, straight stitch each 6 mm from the fold and use a rouleau hook to pull the cord through to the right side.

'Maharani' Cummerbund/Belt

This belt or cummerbund has been designed to go with the patchwork skirt (see page 40), but it could be made to match any items in your wardrobe.

The cummerbund has very little patchwork on it—it is nearly all trapunto. Making it is a good way to learn this technique of cording. Of course a cummerbund can be made without patchwork—you could just embellish it with braids and ribbons if you prefer.

Materials

- Stiff Vilene for lining, 90 cm by 15 cm
- Two pieces, 15 cm of chintz or other material for front and back, 90 cm (or waist measurement plus 15 cm) by 15 cm. If you plan to wear the cummerbund with a skirt use the same material.
- Two pieces of main fabric for rouleau ties, 90 cm by 4 cm.
- 7-ply acrylic macrame cord, one skein (see trapunto instructions on page 18).
- Braids and ribbons (if the belt is to be worn with the skirt, use the same braid and ribbon as you did for the patchwork and bars)
- Bodkin for trapunto
- Rouleau hook
- Two or more macrame beads, two tassels and/or feathers
- Patchwork stripping 15 cm by 20 mm

Method

1 Cut two lengths of material 90 cm long and 15 cm wide for the front and lining of the belt.

Cut two rouleau cords, on the straight, 90 cm by 4 cm.

2 Place one length of fabric, with right side up, on top of the Vilene and stitch 6 mm in from the raw top edge along one length.

3 Stitch eleven channels, each 12 mm wide, as shown in the illustration below.

4 Cut to the desired shape (see illustration below). Thread all the channels with macrame cord using the bodkin (see trapunto instructions on page 18).

5 Flat sew two prejoined pieces of patchwork on an angle (as in the illustration on page 37) to the centre of the cummerbund. Embellish with braids and ribbons.

6 To make the rouleau cords:

Fold the two pieces of fabric for rouleau ties in half lengthwise, with right sides facing in.

Sew along the length with a 10-mm seam allowance.

Pull cords through to the right side by pushing a rouleau hook through to the end and pulling it back so that the seam is inside the cord.

7 Sew rouleau cords for ties, one at each end of the cummerbund. Backstitch over the cord ends a few times to secure them strongly.

Cutting out for cummerbund

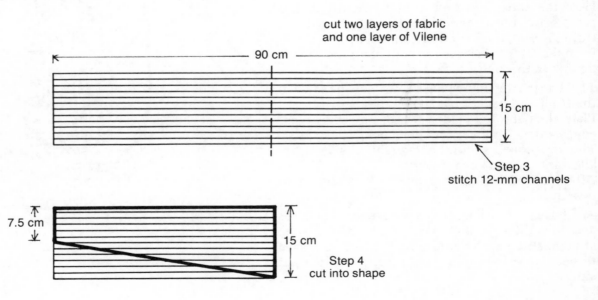

cut two layers of fabric and one layer of Vilene

90 cm

15 cm

Step 3 stitch 12-mm channels

7.5 cm

15 cm

Step 4 cut into shape

Attaching the rouleau cords

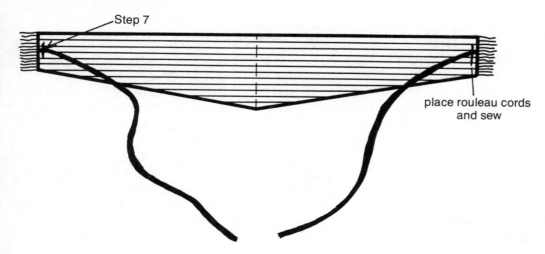

Step 7

place rouleau cords and sew

8 Cut the lining to size. With right sides of cummerbund and lining facing, sew 6-mm seams across the top of the cummerbund. Use the 6-mm line of stitching as a guide.

Turning, sew down the ends, still using 6-mm seams. Make sure the rouleau cord is not caught in the top or bottom seams.

9 Turn again (leaving the machine needle in the fabric while turning will help). Sew across the bottom of the cummerbund leaving an 8-cm gap for turning the cummerbund right side out.

Continue to sew to end.

10 Turn and sew last end and back sew to secure stitching.

Trim off any untidy edges. Snip off across corners to get rid of bulk, but don't cut the stitching.

11 Turn through so that the right sides of the cummerbund are outside and the Vilene is in the centre.

Handsew opening neatly.

12 Finish off with macrame beads and tassels or feathers.

Finished cummerbund

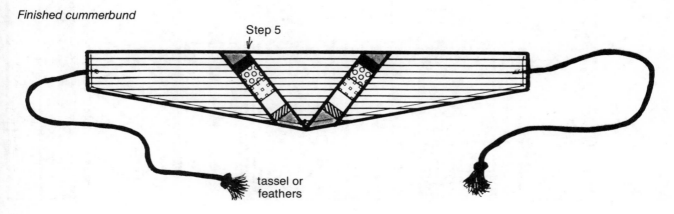

Step 5

tassel or feathers

'Lapis Lazuli' Reversible Poncho

Ponchos are traditionally used as blankets in the Spanish-speaking world, but this poncho has become a high-fashion garment.

It is a good idea to use some of the fabric of the reverse side in the patchwork and also to decorate the plain reverse side. This one has a jewelled phoenix embroidered on the back.

Suggested Fabrics

Chintz, cotton, polycotton, poplin, corduroy and homespun are all suitable.

Materials

- Main fabric for lining, 1.6 metres of 150-cm material or 3 m of 90-cm material
- Patchwork for borders: two sets of stripping for each pattern. The patterns are joined together with colourful bars. The finished piece should measure 1.5 by 1.5 m
- Two buttons or frog fasteners

Important note:
The directions for the lining are given for fabric 150-cm wide, but if you want to use 90-cm fabric, the simplest way is to cut two pieces 1.5 m long and 76 cm wide and join them lengthwise as shown in the illustration on page 39. This seam becomes the shoulder seam.

Method

1 Fold lining material (cut 1.52 m by 1.5 m) in half widthwise, then in quarters.
The material must be folded exactly to mark the centre point on the poncho in preparation for making the neck.

2 To mark neck:
From the centre point of the fold (that is, on the shoulder), mark a point 10 cm across and 5 cm down for the front and back neck.
Mark and cut out the neck in an oval shape as shown in the illustration on page 39.
Unfold the poncho, mark and cut through the centre front from neck to hem.
Fold in half again through centre of poncho to reshape the front neckline.
Mark 25 mm down from the centre front neck edges and cut, as shown in the illustration on page 39. This is to make the front neck lower than the back.

The finished poncho

Cutting out for poncho

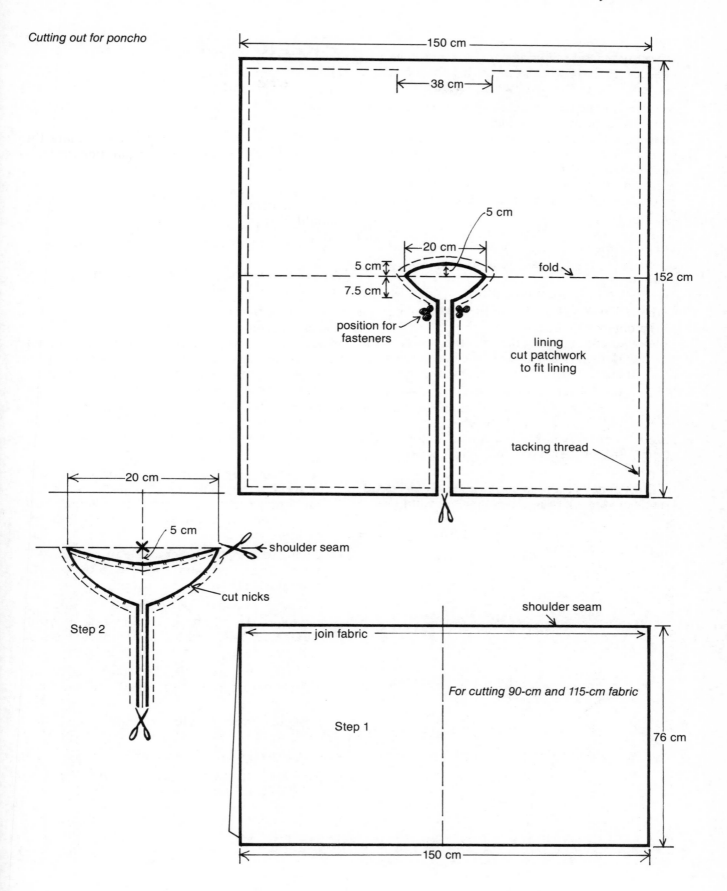

150 cm

38 cm

5 cm

20 cm

5 cm

5 cm

7.5 cm

fold

152 cm

position for fasteners

lining
cut patchwork
to fit lining

tacking thread

20 cm

5 cm

shoulder seam

cut nicks

Step 2

shoulder seam

join fabric

For cutting 90-cm and 115-cm fabric

Step 1

76 cm

150 cm

Note:
If you want to make the poncho reversible, you need to do Step 3 before applying the lining (or reverse side) to the patchwork (Step 2).

3   To make the most of the reversible poncho, you can now decorate the inside.

For the poncho pictured in the colour pages I painted a phoenix on the inside back, then embroidered and beaded it. I finished it off with cornelli embroidery around all edges. (Cornelli embroidery is a corded silk cotton design, machine-sewn, to finish garments.)

You could also choose from the decorations which are available commercially and easy to apply.

4   Place lining on patchwork with right sides together.

Smooth out then pin the right side around as shown in the illustration below, leaving a 38-cm opening at the bottom of the back.

Pin down front opening on both sides and cut the patchwork to match, following the line of the neck. Straight stitch with a 12-mm seam allowance.

5   Repeat sewing line around neck edge to strengthen before cutting small nicks around the neck edge to help the neck curve sit flat.

Snip the corners, making sure you do not cut the straight stitches. This will make the corners of the finished garment less bulky.

6   Turn poncho through to right side and press flat. Handsew the opening to finish off using blind stitch.

Finish the neck at front by handsewing on the buttons or frog fasteners.

'Fireglow' Skirt

The skirt is made in one background colour with a border of patchwork near the hem.

First you need to decide how full your skirt will be. You will have enough patchwork, when it is increased by bars, to give you about 3 m. If you choose not to use bars, you will need to make more patchwork or have a less full skirt.

Note: The cummerbund on page 36 was designed to be worn with this skirt. If you want to make the cummerbund as well you need to check material requirements and buy all the materials at the same time.

The skirt shown measures approximately 3 m around the hem and is 90 cm long.

Suitable Fabrics

Closely woven cotton, poplin, polycotton, home-spun or chintz. (As with all patchwork, fraying can be a problem if you use loosely woven materials.) Taffetas and pinwale velvet can also be used.

Cottons are not only less likely to fray than artificial fibres, they are more in keeping with the traditional nature of this craft. They also form a good base for applying lace, ribbons and braids.

Materials

- For patchwork you will need at least five half-metre lengths of different coloured fabrics. If you want to use up to nine different colours, you would need approximately 30-cm lengths of each.

- If you are going to add embellishment you will need 5 m each of the ribbons, lace braids and other decorations for the stripping.

- For bars you will need to decide how many you need and the length of each to work out your requirements for ribbons, braids and laces. Main fabric requirements include bars.

- For the main fabric of the skirt you will need 2 m of 150-cm material or 4 m of 90-cm or 115-cm material.

- 1 skein 7-ply acrylic macrame cord (for trapunto)

- Bodkin and a long rouleau hook for threading

- For bask (waist band and top panel of skirt): 3-mm elastic, 3 m

Method

1 Cut and sew four sets of stripping with five to nine colours 90 cm long. Extra colours will result in wider borders. For desired widths of strips, follow the patterns on page 12.

Cut eight strips of background fabric 90 cm long and 12.5 cm wide and sew onto outer edges of each set of stripping. This provides the outer edges of the patchwork border.

2 Prepare bars with main fabric. Your style of patchwork will help you decide how many you will need—you can sew them between the sets of patchwork to make up blocks.

Neaten edges to give a completed border about 3 m long.

3 Next prepare the trapunto hem by cutting three 15-cm lengths of 150 cm fabric or four 15-cm lengths of 90 cm fabric.

Join all pieces end to end so that the piece is about 4 m long.

Overlock and neaten the joins and press.

With right sides out, fold in half lengthwise and press.

Straight stitch five channels 13 mm apart, starting at the folded edge, to prepare the channels for cording.

There will be a seam allowance over on the raw edge. Trim this back to 6 mm.

4 You now need to attach the hem to the patchwork border.

With right side of patchwork uppermost, place the channelled hem on top. Keep the raw edges together and straight stitch on top of the last channel to give a 6-mm seam allowance.

Overlock to finish edges and cut off any excess hem.

5 Thread macrame cord through the channels with a bodkin (see trapunto instructions on page 18).

6 To make the bask:

If you are using 150-cm material, cut one length of 33 cm. If you have 90-cm material, cut one piece of 33 cm and one of 60 cm and join the two pieces.

Overlock or zigzag one 150-cm edge.

Press a fold of 7.5 cm, as shown in the illustration above right, on the overlocked edge to make a shirred waist.

Starting at the overlocked edge, sew the edge down and straight stitch the channels 13 mm apart for the elastic to be threaded through at the waist.

7 Cut six 56-cm lengths of 3-mm elastic. Using a bodkin, thread the elastic through the prepared channels, securing the ends with pins.

Backstitch the elastic at each end of the waist to secure.

Mark three notches evenly where shown in the illustration below.

Bask, showing notch positions

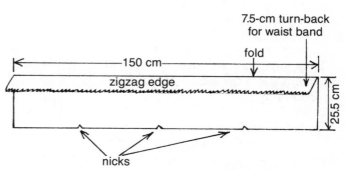

8 To make the middle panel for the skirt:

Cut three 34-cm lengths of 150-cm material or four 34-cm lengths of 90-cm material, or vary the length according to how long you want the finished skirt to be. (Add the width of the patchwork plus hem to the width of the bask and subtract the result from your overall length to find the width you will need for the middle skirt panel.)

Remember the seam allowances—for the middle skirt panel they are 6 mm.

Join fabric, overlock edges to neaten and press.

Important note:
Experience has taught that it is much easier to cut off any excess on the middle skirt panel and trapunto hem after sewing to the patchwork border. The reason for this is that they are cut on the straight grain of the fabric whilst the patchwork border can end up on the bias or at least with lots of joined seams on the edges, so you have to watch, when sewing seams and edges together, that the patchwork border does not stretch as it is sewn. Let the patchwork glide through gently and all is well. Don't overpress the border, either, as this can also make it stretch.

9 The middle skirt now has to be attached to the patchwork and trapunto hem.

Place the patchworked hem right side up with the right side of the middle skirt facing in.

With raw edges together, stitch a 6-mm seam allowance.

Neaten with overlock or zigzag and trim off excess from end of middle skirt.

10 Using a large straight stitch, sew two lines of gather thread 6 mm and 9 mm in from the top edge of the middle skirt.

This gives you a gather edge, so leave threads at the ends long enough to work with. Pull gently to shirr!

Mark three notches evenly across the top of the stitching so that you will have four equal amounts of fabric to sew into the four areas of the bask.

Gently pull the gather threads again so that the skirt is evenly gathered.

Pin notches to notches on bask.

Place several pins through the gathering so that the middle skirt and bask are brought together completely.

Carefully stitch the skirt to the bask, making sure the gathering is straight and even.

Zigzag or overlock to neaten edges.

11 To complete the skirt, the back seam must now be sewn.

Match all seams, from the bask to the middle skirt panel to the patchwork with its trapunto border. Straight stitch and finish with zigzag or overlock to neaten.

Checklist for Skirt

1 Prepare colour coordination.

2 Prepare patchwork.

3 Prepare bars and insert to form a complete patchwork border.

4 Prepare trapunto hem.

5 Attach hem to patchwork band and trim.

6 Prepare bask (waist and top section of skirt).

7 Prepare middle of skirt to desired length.

8 Attach patchwork band with hem to middle skirt and cut excess from middle skirt.

9 Sew bask and middle skirt together after the middle skirt has been trimmed.

10 Finish off skirt.

11 Make cummerbund (page 36) for a finished look.

The completed skirt showing measurements

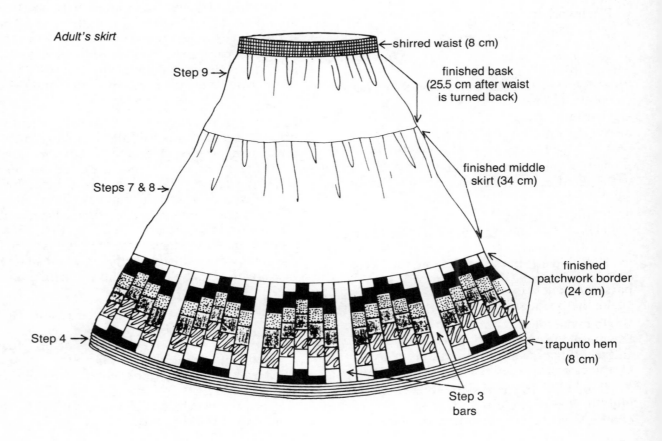

Adult's skirt

Step 9 →

Steps 7 & 8 →

Step 4 →

←shirred waist (8 cm)

finished bask (25.5 cm after waist is turned back)

finished middle skirt (34 cm)

finished patchwork border (24 cm)

←trapunto hem (8 cm)

Step 3 bars

'Denim and Lace' Child's Skirt

(Fits 7–10 year olds)

This girl's skirt can be made for 'best' or from a durable fabric such as denim, as in the photograph in the colour pages.

You may like to make mother-and-daughter matching skirts, as this is basically a smaller, simpler version of the adult skirt.

The directions given are for a skirt for girls between 7 and 10 years, but you can adapt it for other sizes. Make the waist on the bask slightly loose as there are rouleau cords to tie which will give a firm waist. The fullness at the bottom of the skirt is 2.75 m and the length is 66 cm.

If the skirt becomes too small, all you need to do is make a larger bask section. When the skirt can no longer be altered, simply remove the patchwork and use it in some other way. The Seminoles added patchwork to lengthen their children's clothes as they grew and made skirts and pants loose at the waist to allow for growth. They were tied firm with a belt.

Materials

- Patchwork in five colours 90 cm long and 25 cm wide, using the scalloped or angled patchwork designs shown on pages 14–15.
- Main fabric, 2.5 m of 90-cm material
- Laces, braids or ribbons, 2.5 m each for embellishing bars
- Feathers
- 25-mm pregathered lace for hem, 2.5 m
- 3-mm waist elastic, 2 m

Method

1   Make two sets of patchwork stripping with five colours, each cut into widths of 4 cm.

Also cut four strips 8 cm wide in the main fabric for borders.

2   To prepare nine blocks of patchwork:

Make a strip 20 cm long and 75 cm wide for the bars, then cut it into nine 20-cm bars.

Make the border as for the lady's skirt (page 40).

3   To make the trapunto hem, cut three pieces of the main colour 90 cm long and 7 cm wide. Join these end to end with right sides together.

Overlock or zigzag seams to neaten.

With right side facing out, press in half lengthwise and sew three channels, 13 mm wide, starting from folded edge.

Do not thread cords through the channels yet – you need to attach the trapunto to the patchwork first. Sew hem to patchwork border by laying patchwork right side up and placing hem on top. Use the last channel line as a guide for sewing.

Trim excess off raw edges to leave a 6-mm seam allowance.

Cut off any excess trapunto border and neaten with zigzag or overlocking.

4   Thread 7-ply acrylic macrame cord through the three hem channels.

5   To make the middle skirt:

Cut three pieces of background fabric 90 cm long and 32 cm wide. With right sides of fabric facing, join seams through the width.

Neaten with overlock or zigzag.

Place middle skirt section with right side facing right side of patchwork. Allow 6-mm seams and sew patchwork to middle skirt.

Overlock or zigzag to neaten and cut off excess middle skirt.

6   To make the bask (waist band and top panel) of the skirt:

Cut main fabric 90 cm long and 23 cm wide.

Zigzag or overlock one 90-cm edge.

Fold overlocked hem back 5 cm with right sides out and press.

Sew four channels across the width, 13 mm apart, for the waist, starting at the overlocked edge.

Cut four lengths of elastic 45 cm long, secure them at one end then thread them through the channels. Sew the other ends to secure.

Making the bask for child's skirt

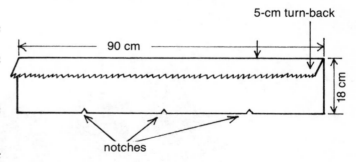

5-cm turn-back

90 cm

18 cm

notches

7   To join bask and middle skirt:

Mark and notch the raw bottom edge of the bask into four even sections.

Mark and notch the top edge of the middle skirt into four even sections.

You will notice that the middle skirt has a much greater circumference, so the next step is to sew gather lines across the top of the middle skirt, so that the two pieces can be eased together.

Using large stitches, straight sew 6 mm in from the top edge.

For strong gather thread repeat, this time sewing 10 mm from the edge.

Pull both gather threads at the same time until the gathered edge fits the bask edge.

Lay right sides of bask and middle skirt together with gathered edges up.

Pin between notches and sew 10 mm in from the edge, carefully manipulating the gathering as you go.

Finish off edge with zigzag or overlock.

8 Sew pregathered lace around the bottom of the hem on the wrong side, sewing along the seam line created for the bottom channel so that the lace just peeps out from the bottom edge.

9 Match back seam of skirt, making sure waist, middle skirt, patchwork and hem seams meet exactly.

Pin then stitch. Overlock or zigzag to neaten.

10 To make rouleau cords, cut two pieces of main fabric 90 cm long and 4 cm wide.

Fold in half lengthwise with right sides facing in and stitch 6 mm in from the raw edges.

To turn right side out, pull through with rouleau hook.

Using rouleau hook, pull beads onto cord.

Insert three or four feathers in the rouleau cord and back stitch to secure.

Tie a knot at the end of the cord next to the feathers and pull beads back onto the knot.

Sew the cords to the side of the skirt waist.

Finished child's skirt

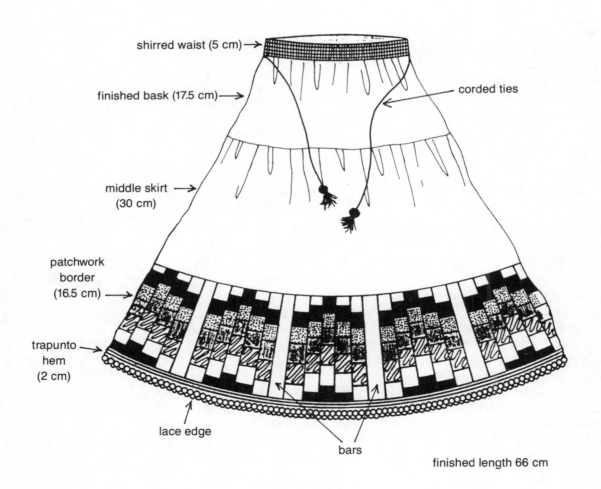

shirred waist (5 cm)

finished bask (17.5 cm)

corded ties

middle skirt (30 cm)

patchwork border (16.5 cm)

trapunto hem (2 cm)

lace edge

bars

finished length 66 cm

44

'Pacific Jewel' Kimono Jacket

This jacket is one-size-fits-all, with wide sleeves that on different wearers will reach different places between elbow and wrist. The jacket's finished length is 97 cm. You can create your own paper pattern using the given pattern and increasing all measurements to the required amount. If you are making the jacket for someone very large or very small, make adjustments on your paper pattern first so material is not wasted. The only easy alteration for different sizes is under the arm and down the side seam.

This style of jacket suits men and women, but most men will prefer less embellishment.

Materials

- For body of jacket and trapunto edging, 3 m of 150-cm material or 4 m of 90-cm material.
- Patchwork stripping, 1 m long and 30 cm wide for front border and 45 cm long and 28 cm wide for back (so you will need two sets of stripping). Choose seven colours each 10 cm wide and 90 cm long
- 7-ply acrylic macrame cord for trapunto pockets, cuffs and border, 1 skein
- A bodkin
- 25-mm braid for finishing patchwork edges, 3 m
- Ribbons and braids to embellish bars and patchwork, 2 m
- 1 tassel for back panel point if desired

Method

1 Use the measurements to create your own paper pattern.

Fold fabric and cut fronts and back. Cut two pieces exactly the same, both with centre fold through front and back. Cut through centre fold on one layer only from neck to bottom hem to make two front pieces.

Mark notches on sides for pocket position. (*Note:* you will be recutting front neck later.) Mark and notch the centre of the back neck.

Recut the front neck, using the measurements shown.

2 To make patchwork:

you can use two panels, each 1 m long and 15 cm wide, with a piece about 45 cm long and 28 cm wide for the back of the jacket.

Alternatively, you can make a piece of patchwork 1 m long and 20 cm wide and splice it through the centre lengthwise (as I have done in the kimono jacket pictured in the colour pages). You would then use half each for the left and right fronts so that the colours flow from one side to the other.

Again, you will need a separate piece of patchwork to add a splash of colour to the back.

3 Bars can also be made and added, though if the jacket is being made for a man, you will have to keep his taste in mind (many men will prefer to have a less ornate jacket, so you could eliminate embellishments on the bars).

4 To make the trapunto trims, see page 18 for detailed instructions.

You will need to curve the front trapunto bands at the bottom to give a nicely finished look, as shown in the illustration below. Mark and cut curved bottom edges. Sew with right sides facing in and a 6-mm seam allowance. Turn out to right side, press, then continue to stitch channels.

For front and neck bands, cut two pieces 12 cm wide.

For the pocket bands cut two pieces 23 cm long and 13 cm wide.

For sleeve bands or cuffs cut two pieces 50 cm long and 15 cm wide.

Prepare all bands by folding in half lengthwise with right sides facing out and pressing. Then start from the folded edge and straight stitch 12-mm channels, remembering that the front bottom edges need to be curved.

Trim back all raw edges neatly to a 10-mm seam allowance and neaten off.

Front and neck bands for kimono jacket
The bottom edges of the trapunto channels curve inwards to give a neat finish to the jacket.

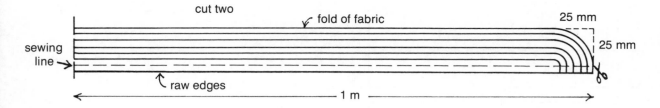

Cutting out for kimono jacket

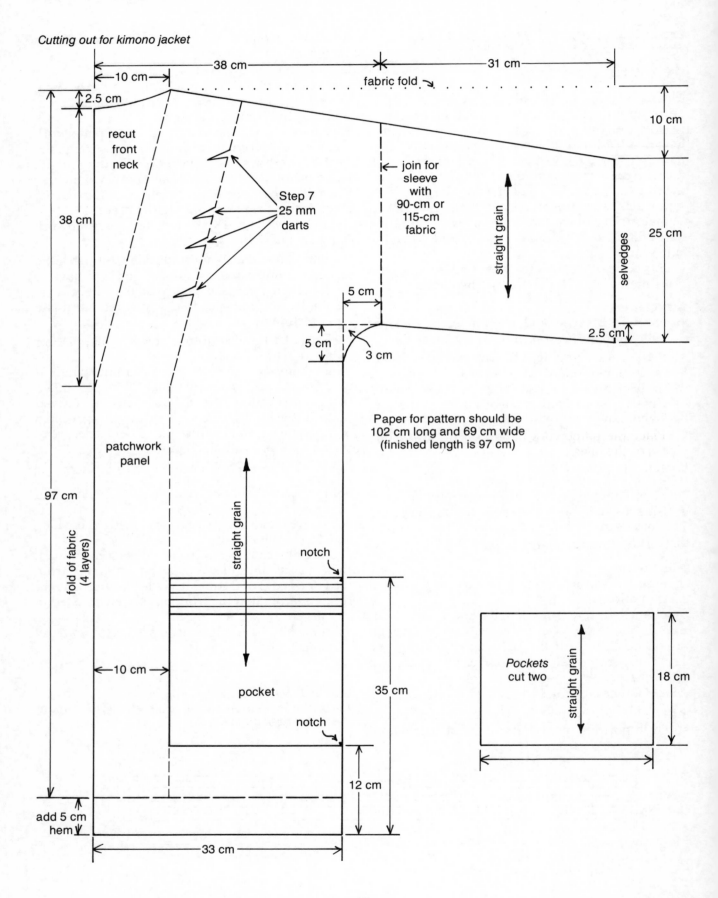

10 cm

38 cm

31 cm

fabric fold

2.5 cm

recut
front
neck

10 cm

38 cm

Step 7
25 mm
darts

join for
sleeve
with
90-cm or
115-cm
fabric

straight grain

25 cm

selvedges

5 cm

5 cm

2.5 cm

3 cm

97 cm

fold of fabric
(4 layers)

patchwork
panel

Paper for pattern should be
102 cm long and 69 cm wide
(finished length is 97 cm)

straight grain

10 cm

notch

pocket

35 cm

notch

12 cm

add 5 cm
hem

33 cm

Pockets
cut two

straight grain

18 cm

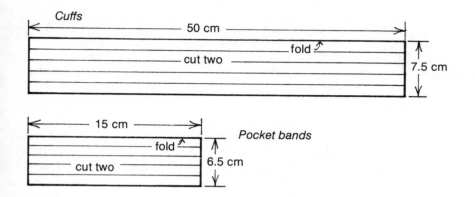

Cuffs

50 cm

fold

cut two

7.5 cm

15 cm

Pocket bands

fold

cut two

6.5 cm

5 Cut two pockets 18 cm long and 23 cm wide as shown opposite.

6 Make four trapunto channels in pocket bands. To sew bands to pockets place raw edges together with right sides facing inwards.
Straight stitch on the wrong side of the band, with a 6-mm seam allowance.
Thread bodkin with acrylic macrame cord and finish off the bands with trapunto.
Overlock and zigzag sides and bottom of pockets to neaten edges.
Hand tack hem 6 mm up from the bottom.

7 Place the patchwork panels on the two front pieces of the jacket.
Pin on inner edges then straight stitch from bottom edge to top shoulder with a 6-mm seam allowance.
On outer edges of patchwork panels, pin from hem up about 56 cm.
You will need to fit the patchwork carefully up to the shoulder as there will be excess fabric.
To do this, dart or pin every second patchwork seam an extra 6 mm in from the edge, running it in from about 25 mm to nothing, moving towards the centre of the patchwork panel and ending up on an existing seam. Make more darts if necessary.
These darts help to curve the patchwork. Repeat this procedure about four times, or until the panel of patchwork sits smoothly up to the shoulder seam.
With the excess fabric taken in on the seams on the outer edge of the patchwork piece, pin and straight stitch in position along outer edge of patchwork panel, 10 mm in from raw edges.
Trim off untidy edges to neaten.

8 Place inner edge of pocket next to the patchwork, using the notches on the sides to make sure the two pockets are level. Straight stitch down this edge. (This raw edge will be hidden with braid at the same time as the edge of the patchwork panel.)
Sew across hem of pocket.

Cut any excess fabric at side seam of pockets. Straight stitch along side seam of jacket fronts. Repeat for other pocket.

9 Prepare back of jacket by placing the patchwork panel directly in the centre, using the notch at the centre back neck to make sure it is centred.
Pin in place, then straight stitch into position around edges.
Trim all edges to neaten.

10 On the back of the jacket, place 25-mm braid over the raw edges of the patchwork and straight stitch on outside edge of braid, starting at the right shoulder edge.
When you reach your first turning point, make sure you leave the machine needle down, through the braid and the fabric. Lift the presser foot on the machine and swivel the fabric so that the stitches will go in the new direction.
Lower the presser foot and continue to sew. This will give you a neat mitred corner point. Continue stitching all outside edges.
Sew inner edge of braid next, starting at the right shoulder edge.
When you reach the corner, pin to staple down a neat mitre pleat as shown in the illustration below, and repeat the procedure with the presser foot.

Mitred edges of patchwork

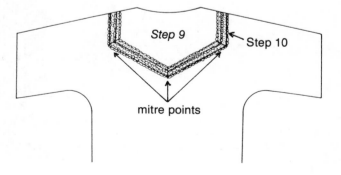

Step 9

Step 10

mitre points

11 For the jacket fronts, cover the raw edges of the patchwork fronts with 25-mm braid and remember that the braid also needs to cover the raw edges on the pocket. Straight stitch both sides of the braid to the fronts.

Pin front shoulder seams to back shoulder seam. Straight stitch the shoulders, then zigzag or overlock to neaten.

12 Place prepared cuff bands on sleeve edges with right sides facing in and straight stitch, then neaten with zigzag or overlock.

Using the bodkin and macrame cording, thread the five channels.

13 Pin the back and front side seams, making sure they meet exactly at hem, cuffs and armpit. Make sure the pocket edges are included—they must be sewn into the side seams.

Straight stitch from the bottom hem of the jacket, continuing up through the armpit and down the sleeve to the end of the cuffs.

Zigzag or overlock to finish neatly.

Repeat on second side.

14 First overlock or zigzag the raw edge of the hem.

Next, the trapunto bands need to be attached to the jacket. As with the sleeves, they are attached first and threaded later.

There is a 5-cm hem allowance on the jacket. Mark 5 cm on the fronts of the jacket and place the curved end of the left front band at this mark. Pin the left front band into position.

15 Straight sew from the fifth channel (remember to leave the channel ends open so the cord can be threaded through later).

Straight stitch up the left front and across the neck to the notch marked at the back of the neck.

Cut off excess band, leaving 2 cm to spare. Cut exactly the same amount from the other band so that the two bands are identical.

Pin precut band into position—continue sewing to curved bottom edge.

Overlock or zigzag the edges to neaten.

Thread the bodkin with acrylic macrame cord and thread the cord through the channels until all are threaded on both sides.

16 Pin and stitch trapunto bands together at back of neck.

Trim seam to 5 mm then overlock or zigzag.

Handsew a piece of 12-mm ribbon along the join at the neck to neaten. Straight stitch along band over this join. Zigzag or overlock to neaten.

17 Straight stitch the threaded curved bands into place at the bottom of the jacket.

Bring the 5-cm hem back over the curved edge of the band. Sew together, then overlock or zigzag to neaten edges.

Turn the corner out so that the curved band sits flush at the bottom corner of the hem.

Repeat on the other side.

18 Press bottom hem up 5 cm all around to coincide with the two front bands.

Use hem stitch, blind stitch or herringbone to finish off the kimono jacket.

Finished kimono jacket

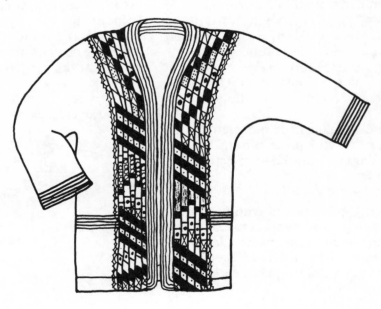

'Aquamarine' Apache top. *This casual top can be worn for day or evening in all four seasons.*

Inset: The 'Nomad' Apache bag *can be made to match any outfit. It has a handy pocket inside for small items.*

The 'Persian Jewel' collection. *The Seminole patchwork blind is
unlined so that the light can shine through it to give the effect
of leadlight.*
The 'Arrowhead' wallhanging *is embellished with jewels and feathers.
The bookmark and hatband can be made from spare scraps of patchwork.*

'Mischief' Tabard Jacket

This long, tunic-style jacket is based on the tabards worn by medieval knights.

Since the tabard has a mixture of three patchwork designs, this is your chance to have lots of fun blending and playing with colour and design.

Materials

- For the patchwork you will need about eight different colours, in strips 50 cm long of about 1 m widths (this will make 4 m of contrasting colours) and about 2.5 m of the main background.

- Extra main colour fabric for trapunto at sides and hem, 1m

- Lining material, 90 cm wide and 2.5 m long. This can be the same as the main colour, or a contrasting or complementary colour.
  If using the main fabric as the lining, you need a total of 6.25 m.

- Braid, 5 m

- Ribbon or lace, 5 m

- Six fancy tassels: four for joining sides and two for shoulder finish

Method

1 Make a paper pattern to fit from the illustrations on page 50. Use the pattern to cut out the linings as shown in the illustration.

2 Sew five sets of stripping with three to five colours for each patchwork design, including the main colour blended in occasionally.
Zigzag or overlock edges and press.
Embellish with ribbons or braid.
Piece the patchwork in widths of 1.3 m in the angled, scalloped and zigzag different designs or in designs of your choice.
Add and sew strips of the main colour between each pattern.

3 Join each border with a strip of main colour fabric 7.5 cm wide to form a large piece of patchwork about 1 m long and 1.3 m wide.

4 Press patchwork as you go, then press the whole piece when step 3 has been completed.
Lay the lining on pieced patchwork, with right sides together.
Make sure that the lining for back and fronts is going in the same direction and that the tops and bottoms of the back and front patchwork sections align.
Pin lining carefully to patchwork and cut the patchwork to match the lining exactly.

5 Fold the back of the tabard in half lengthwise and notch centre neck on both the lining and the patchwork piece.
Remove pins to separate lining from patchwork.
Join shoulders with straight stitch.
First sew linings, then sew patchwork fronts and back together across the shoulder seams, with a 6-mm seam allowance.
Overlock or zigzag to neaten.

6 To make the trapunto bands to finish off the front opening of the tabard:
Cut two bands 1.5 m long and 15 cm wide.
Fold and stitch channels.
The lower edges need to be curved (as for the kimono jacket).
Do not thread the acrylic cord through yet, as this will make the piece difficult to sew neatly at the seams.

Bands for tabard jacket

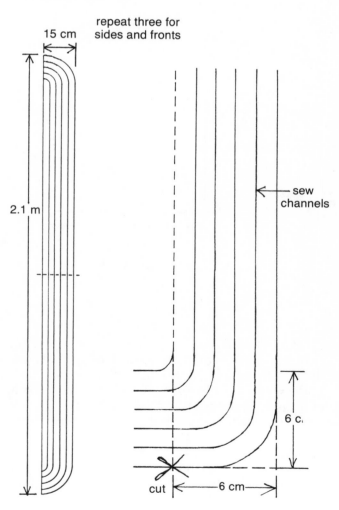

Cutting out for tabard jacket

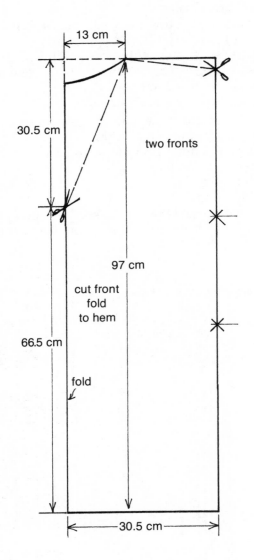

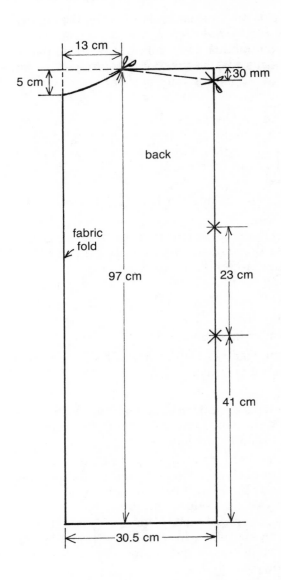

7 Pin bands to pieced patchwork fronts, starting with the curved edge of the band 13 mm up from the bottom of the front hem.

The last stitched channel you sew should be 6 mm in from the raw edges. Use the stitching channel as a guideline when sewing the bands to the fronts. Start above the fifth channel but leave the channels open at the ends.

Finish sewing the band around the neck edge then to the notch at the centre back.

Do not sew down at the very bottom or at the centre back—this will be done after the channels have been corded.

Important note:

Leave 2 cm extra band at centre back and cut off excess.

Repeat with right front band, cutting the same amount of excess band off first before sewing.

Overlock or zigzag to neaten.

8   Cord all channels on both bands, making sure there is no puckering or pulling of fabric.

Sew curved bottom edge as shown in the illustration on page 45 and overlock to neaten.

Pin bands together at back neck seam, matching the centre notches, and sew seam exactly in the centre.

Make sure the neck band is sitting neatly.

Trim off excess from bands, leaving a 6-mm seam allowance, and finish by overlocking or zigzag.

You can then neaten the back of the neck by hand sewing 13-mm satin ribbon over the back seam of the band. Fold it in under overlocked seam and sew.

9   To make the trapunto bands:

Cut four bands 1 m long and 13 cm wide.

Stitch channels with curved bottom edges but do not cord them yet.

The directions here are the same as for the front bands, but the side bands meet at the shoulder seam.

Start at the curved end of the bands 13 mm from the bottom hem.

Make sure all the curved bands are on the same direct line of patchwork. When sewn, cord the channels.

Finish off the shoulders and join with 12-mm satin ribbon in the same way as suggested for the back neck, covering the overlocked seam.

10   Pin lining to the patchwork with right sides facing in. All bands will be hidden inside the two layers.

Pin directly on the sewing line of the bands, using this line as a guide.

Start pinning on side of tabard, about 45 cm from the hem, and go right up to the shoulder and down the sides, across the bottom hem, up one front and down the other, across the hem and up and over the shoulder down to about 25 cm from the bottom, leaving an opening of about 30 cm to turn the tabard through.

Straight stitch seams and trim excess.

11   Turn tabard through to right side.

Press all seams and close opening with blind stitch.

12   To make a 12-mm pleat on the shoulder seam:

Measure and mark 25 mm from the edge of the patchwork on the shoulder seam, then measure another 25 mm from that mark.

Make a fold between the two marks and place a pin at that point on the shoulder seam. Sew the sides of the pleat up and over both sides of the shoulder seam to secure and handstitch the pleat with the fold facing towards the neck.

Place shoulder pads if required.

Trim each shoulder with a tassel if required.

13   Measure 30 cm down the side seams from the shoulder seam on both front and back.

Pin together to make the armhole.

Pin 23 cm down from the underarm on back and front.

Pin and secure to make a short side seam with a split up from the hem.

14   On both spots where pins are placed, hand-stitch about 13 mm over and over to make it secure. Sew a tassel on each of these spots.

Finished tabard jacket

51

'Aquamarine' Apache Top

This is a version of the universal pull-on shirt, open at the neck, worn by North American Indians. The Apache top is colourfully decorated with ribbons, braid and feathers.

Suggested Fabrics

Chintz, cotton, homespun, leatherette, pinwale corduroy, poplin or velvet.

Materials

- Main fabric—2 m of 150-cm, 2.5 m of 115-cm or 3 m of 90-cm wide material
- Patchwork for front panel approximately 40 cm by 30 cm
- Braid or ribbon for finishing edges on patchwork panel, 1.5 m
- A small amount (about 160 cm) of acrylic macrame cord for pocket trim only
- A bodkin
- 3 mm elastic, 3 m

Method

1   Prepare patchwork piece to feature on front of Apache top. You can make this in any patchwork style.

2   Prepare paper pattern as shown on page 53.

Important note:
While many of the lessons in this book suggest that you cut a piece of fabric just before using it, it is easier with this garment if you make paper patterns and cut out all the pieces first. Then you can do the same procedure, such as sewing channels, to all the pieces that require it at once.

3   Cut out front and back together. Pin selvedge to selvedge and mark as shown in the illustration on page 53.
Fold back and front in half lengthwise and mark and notch the centre for the neck opening. Mark again 10 cm either side of the centre point to give a 20-cm neck opening.
Mark 25 mm down from the centre point for the back neck opening and 10 cm down from centre for front, making a nice curve. Cut to complete neck opening, as shown in the illustration on page 53.

4   The sleeves are cut 40 cm long, regardless of the width of your material. Fold across from selvedge to selvedge, then fold in half lengthwise. This becomes the centre fold of the sleeve (see illustration on page 53).

5   Lay the paper pattern, pin the four layers together, then cut all together for sleeves.

6   Measure, mark and cut the hip band, sleeve and pocket cuffs and rouleau cords.
Sleeve cuffs—cut two 45 cm by 12 cm (see illustration on page 53).
Pocket and cuffs—cut two 20 cm by 12 cm.
Hip band—cut 150 cm by 15 cm as shown in the illustration on page 53.
Rouleau cord—cut 90 cm by 30 mm.

7   To prepare all the cuffs for trapunto:
Fold cuffs in half and press.
Fold hipband and press as illustrated.
Fold pocket cuffs as illustrated.
Stitch channels 13 mm apart, starting at the fold and working out towards the raw edges.
Do not thread the trapunto yet—it is always done after the channelled piece has been sewn to the garment.

8   Sew cuffs to pockets and overlock or zigzag raw edges.
Using a bodkin, thread cord through channels on pocket cuffs.
Zigzag or overlock sides and bottoms of pockets to neaten.

9   To apply patchwork panel to front of Apache top:
Mark the centre front of the panel by folding in half and marking with chalk or pencil.
Pin the panel first and use the fold to guide you. Straight stitch into position with topsewing.
The raw edges must be covered with braid or ribbon to obtain a neat finish, as in the Apache top pictured in the colour pages.

Important note:
When covering raw edges with braid, always sew the outside edges of the ribbon or braid first so that you can mitre the inside edge (as shown on page 47. Remember to leave the needle down through the fabric as you lift the presser foot to turn corners to give a neat point. Repeat the same method as you sew the inside edge of ribbon or braid, keeping the needle through the fabric and making a pleat or tuck.

10   Place the pockets either side over the corners of the patchwork.
Turn in hem on the centre front edges of each pocket and tack, then position on right side of the front, laying the raw edges of the pocket on the raw edges of the sides and bottom of the front.
Pin and stitch around all three sides, straight stitching down side seam, along the bottom hem, then up the inside of the pocket over the tacking.
Backstitch 25-mm on pocket cuff.

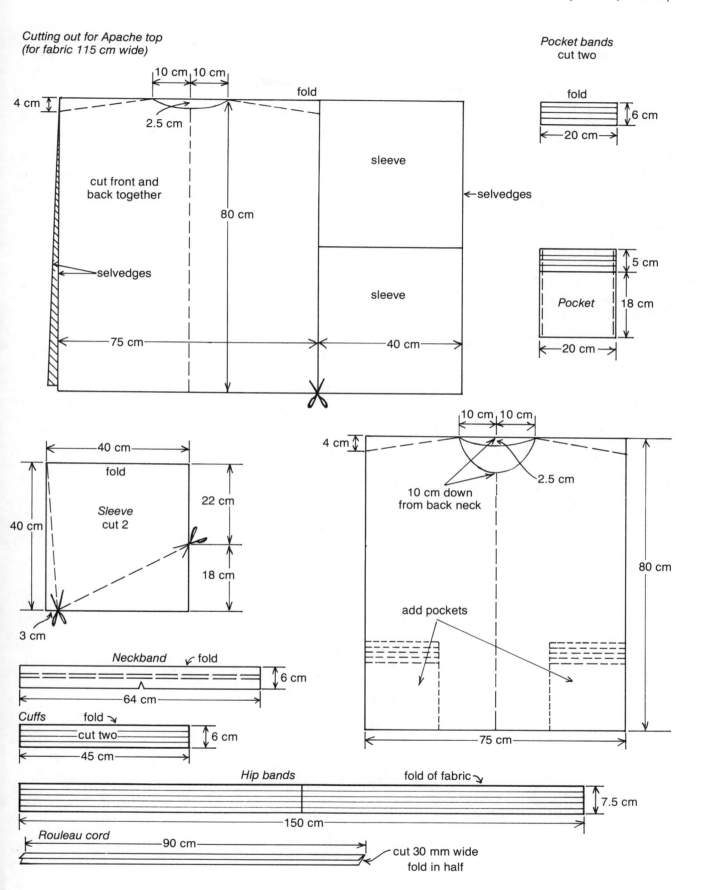

Cutting out for Apache top
(for fabric 115 cm wide)

10 cm | 10 cm

fold

4 cm

2.5 cm

cut front and
back together

80 cm

sleeve

←selvedges

selvedges

sleeve

75 cm

40 cm

Pocket bands
cut two

fold

6 cm

20 cm

5 cm

Pocket

18 cm

20 cm

40 cm

fold

Sleeve
cut 2

40 cm

22 cm

18 cm

3 cm

10 cm | 10 cm

4 cm

2.5 cm

10 cm down
from back neck

80 cm

add pockets

75 cm

Neckband fold

6 cm

64 cm

Cuffs   fold

cut two

6 cm

45 cm

Hip bands   fold of fabric

7.5 cm

150 cm

Rouleau cord   90 cm

cut 30 mm wide
fold in half

11 Pin and sew back and front shoulder seams together and overlock or zigzag to finish edges.

12 Mark notches on top centres of sleeves, matching the notches to shoulder seam.
Pin sleeves into position with right sides of bodice and sleeves facing in.
Straight stitch sleeves with a 10-mm seam allowance. Overlock or zigzag raw edges.
Topstitch sleeves 6 mm in from seam to give a neat finish.

13 Measure the neck (it will be about 64 cm) and try it over your head. If it is not big enough, cut front neck at lowest front point another 12 mm. Then cut the neck band to fit the circumference of the neck, allowing 25 mm extra for hems on the front opening of neck band. Overlock edges first then turn the hems back 12 mm and straight stitch hems.

14 Fold neck band in half widthwise.
Starting at the folded edge, measure in 25 mm and straight stitch the first side of the rouleau channel. Measure 12 mm in from this line and straight stitch again to form the complete channel for the rouleau cord.
Next, straight stitch in from raw edges.

15 Find centre of front neck and notch.
Pin neck band to coordinate with notches and with right sides facing in, straight stitch into place, sewing on inside of neckband. Zigzag or overlock to neaten.

16 To prepare rouleau cord:
Fold fabric lengthwise with right sides facing in and straight stitch a seam 6 mm in from raw edges.
Using a steel rouleau hook, pull through to right side.
Using a bodkin, thread the rouleau cord through the channel on the neck band.
Use the rouleau hook to thread macrame beads, then place the hook on the cord and pull the cord through the centre of the bead as shown on page 19. Repeat on the other end of the cord, tying a knot on each end to hold the bead on.

17 Sew cuffs to sleeves and overlock or zigzag to neaten.
Cut six pieces of elastic 13–15 cm long (measure wrists to check length).
Thread every alternate channel only to give a softer feel and finish.
Backstitch the elastics in place on the side seams to secure.

18 Pin and sew side seams from sleeve cuff to bottom of Apache top, leaving one side with a 25-mm opening at the hip. Overlock or zigzag to neaten.
Pin and sew bottom hip band to top with right sides together. Overlock or zigzag to neaten.
Thread elastic through every alternate channel, backstitching elastics in place.
Close side seam by straight stitching then overlock or zigzag.

Finished 'Apache' top

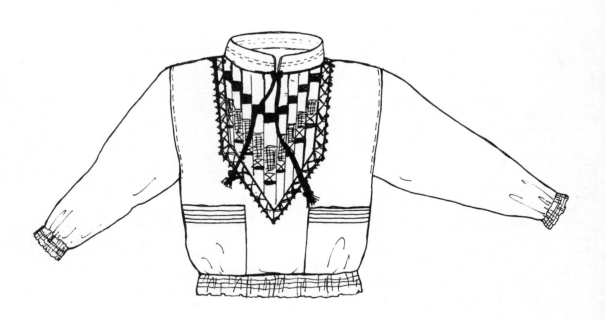

54

Blinds and Wallhangings

'Leadlight' Blind

This blind is unlined so that the light can shine through it to give the effect of leadlight. It measures 171 cm long and 94 cm wide (including tabs and fringe). You will need to adapt the measurements if you want to fit an existing window.

Materials

- Patchwork: for the top panel of the blind you need two sets of stripping, each approximately 90 cm long and 15 cm wide, each of nine colours.
  For the lower panel you need two sets of stripping, each approximately 90 cm long and 15 cm wide, of eight colours.
- Main background material, 4.5 m of 90-cm material
- Braid for bars, 3.2 m
- Macrame beads, 192 (forty-eight each of four different colours).

Method

1 Follow the graph on page 56 and allowing for 6-mm seams on each side of the strip, cut then sew the two sets of patchwork stripping in the scalloped style (see page 14).

2 Press seams all one way then embellish with ribbon or braid, keeping the two sets identical. (You will need to fold in half lengthways and cut carefully through two layers.)

3 To cut black bars, cut two pieces 7.5 cm wide and 1.4 m long, and two pieces 6.3 cm wide and 1.4 m long.
Notice that the main fabric for the top and bottom is about 8 cm longer than needed. This is to allow for balancing and juggling your layout with the scalloped patchwork.
The bars, too, are 18 cm longer than the blind to allow for juggling and adjusting the patchwork pattern.

4 Follow the graph on page 56 to recut stripping. (You will need to fold in half lengthways and cut carefully through two layers.) Overlock or zigzag to neaten edges. As you cut your patchwork strips, lay them and your bars in order across a table.
Sew strips in the scalloped design.
Separate the blind into three sections to sew, then join the three sections together with the larger bars. Overlock or zigzag all seams to neaten.
Embellish the 7.5 cm bars with braid, sewing the braid right next to the seam on either side of each bar. The edge of the braid will show up a little more with the colour sections behind it.

5 To prepare trapunto:
You need two trapunto bands to go down the sides of the blind in the background colour. Cut two pieces of the main background fabric 12.5 cm wide and 1.2 m long.
You need a trapunto band for the top of the blind. Cut one piece 12.5 cm wide and 97 cm long to cover the top of the blind, with an extra 25 mm allowed for turn-back hems on either side.
For nine trapunto tabs for the top of the blind, cut one piece of fabric 1.4 m by 11 cm.

6 To make up the sides of the blind and the top, fold fabric in half lengthwise with right sides facing out.
Press along fold and straight sew channels, starting 12 mm in from the pressed, folded edge.
Sew four channels on all strips.
Trim back raw edges to 5-mm seam allowances. Remember — don't thread the cords yet!

7 Sew trapunto bands to both sides of patchwork piece and neaten then thread cord through channels.
With right side of patchwork uppermost, place trapunto edge on top and sew 5 mm in from the edges, using the last channel as a guideline. Neaten the edges with zigzag or overlock.

8 Thread bodkin with acrylic macrame cord and feed through the four channels on both sides. Repeat for the top of the blind.
You will have 12 mm extra at the ends of the trapunto band on top of the blind. This is for a small turn-back of the hem on each side.

9 Taking the fabric cut for the tabs (140 cm by 11 cm), fold lengthwise with right sides facing in. Sew 5 mm in from raw edges and turn fabric through to right side. Press seam.
Starting from the fold, sew four channels 12 mm apart.
Thread cord through each channel with a bodkin. Cut into nine equal lengths of 15 cm each.
Fold in half lengthwise to make tabs and sew raw edges together. Overlock or zigzag to neaten.
Place the tabs equal distances apart at the back of the top trapunto edge of the blind.
Sew tabs on using the top channel as your sewing guideline.

'Leadlight' blind 6-mm seam allowance
138 cm long and 94 cm wide (not including tabs or fringe)

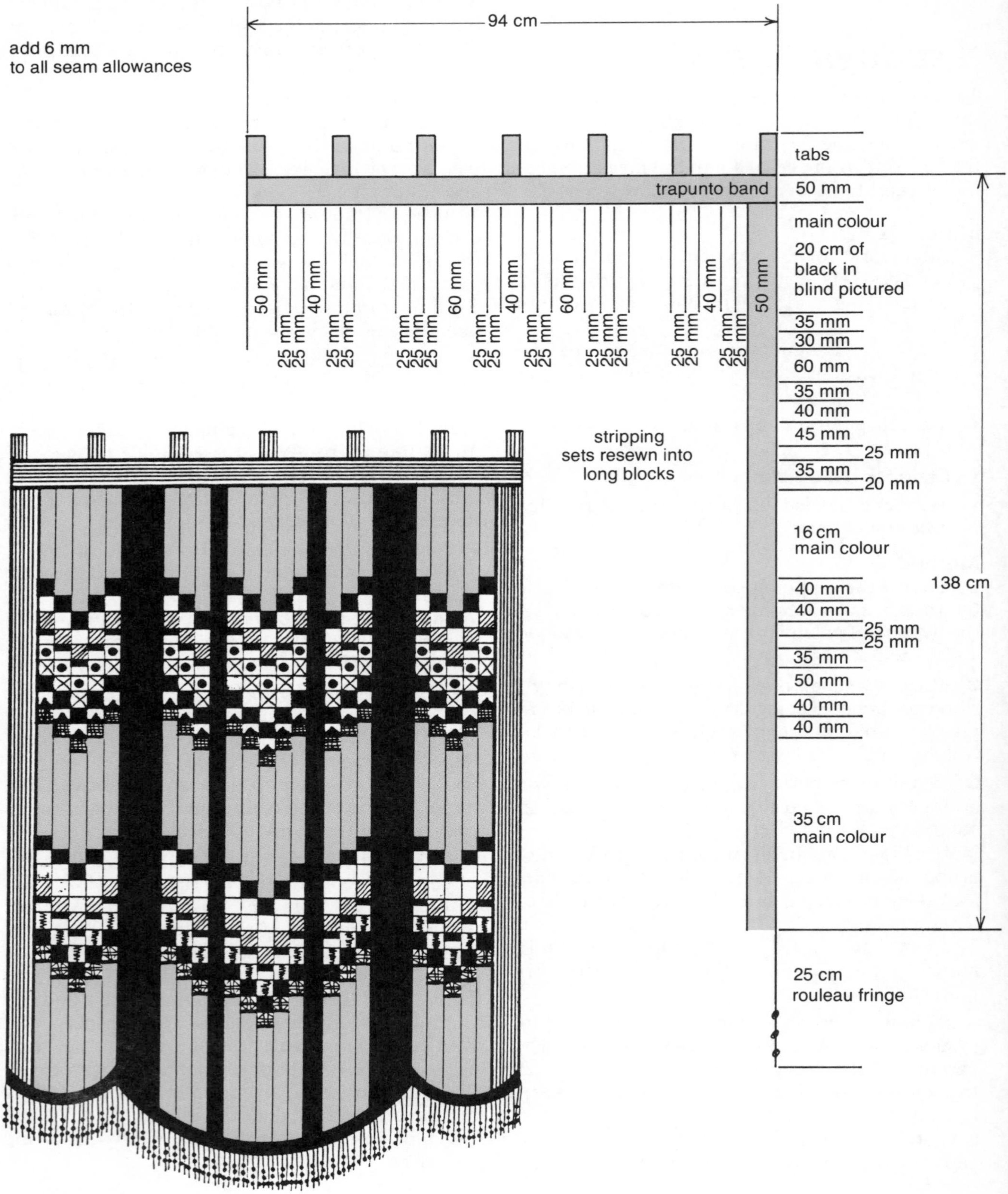

add 6 mm
to all seam allowances

|← —————————————— 94 cm —————————————— →|

tabs

trapunto band — 50 mm

main colour

20 cm of
black in
blind pictured

35 mm
30 mm
60 mm
35 mm
40 mm
45 mm
          25 mm
35 mm
          20 mm

16 cm
main colour

40 mm
40 mm
          25 mm
          25 mm
35 mm
50 mm
40 mm
40 mm

35 cm
main colour

50 mm

stripping
sets resewn into
long blocks

50 mm ... 25 mm ... 40 mm ... 25 mm ... 25 mm ... 60 mm ... 40 mm ... 25 mm ... 25 mm ... 60 mm ... 25 mm ... 40 mm ... 25 mm

138 cm

25 cm
rouleau fringe

10 Measure carefully to scallop your hem (use a plate for a template to help get even curves). Mark and cut.

11 Cut a piece of background fabric 99 cm by 25 cm for facing the bottom of the blind.
Lay the fabric under the bottom edge of the blind and cut the scallops to match exactly.
Sew a small hem on the side edges of the facing.

12 Before sewing the facing to the blind, you need to pin the rouleau cords in place for fringe trim.
To make rouleaus:
You will need forty-eight strips of background fabric 25 cm long and 3 cm wide.
Fold in half lengthwise with right sides facing in. Sew 6 mm in from raw edges and pull through to right side with a rouleau hook.
Pin the rouleau cords 20 mm apart then stitch in place on scalloped edge. You need to sew the facing on after the rouleau cords are in place so that the cords will be sewn on like a fringed edge, upside down on the right side of the blind, 6 mm in from the bottom edge.
Place the right side of the facing onto the right side of the blind and pin around the scalloped edges, making sure that all rouleau cords are tucked away from the edges (otherwise they may get caught up in the seams).
Sew 10 mm in from the edges, right across the bottom of each scallop.
Cut tiny nicks around all the curves, being careful not to snip the stitching. It is a good idea to sew two lines of stitching on the curved edges.

13 Turn the facing to the wrong side of the blind. Neaten the edge of the facing with a 3-mm hem before handsewing the sides of the facing neatly to the sides of the blind.
Catch the top edges of the facing to the blind in a few places.

14 You can thread four beads onto each of the rouleau cords with a rouleau hook. Tie a knot on the ends of the cords.

15 Now that the blind is completed, find a suitable rod to thread through the tabs.
You will probably find that you have some patchwork left over. This is unavoidable since you need approximately one and a half sets, however, patchwork is never wasted! Use it to colour coordinate something else in the room with the blind, such as a pillow case, bookmarks, antimacassars or table mats.

'Arrowhead' Wallhanging

These instructions are for a wallhanging 99 cm long (from top to bottom point) and 50 cm wide, with 75-mm drop tabs which give extra length.

Materials
- Patchwork size will depend on the widths of the fabrics prepared for stripping, but about 76 cm should allow for adjustment. You will need seven colours each of 10-cm wide strips of 150-cm material or seven colours each of 10-cm wide strips of 90-cm material
- Background fabric, 2.5 m of 90-cm material or 2.1 m of 150-cm material (chintz was chosen for the wallhanging picture in the colour pages.
- Silk fringe, 1.7 m
- Braid, 8 m
- One silk tassel
- Jewels, thirty-six
- Macrame beads, ten
- Rouleau cords, four, 46 cm long
- Rouleau hook
- Brass or wooden rod 70 cm long and approximately 30 mm in diameter

Method
1 Prepare two sets of stripping 150 cm long and approximately 50 cm wide.

2 Press seams one way on the stripping.
Embellish with braids or laces to highlight.

Important note:
Bars are added to highlight. Be precise when cutting and sewing so that when you place the mirror-finish blocks together they match perfectly.
Bars must always be cut longer than the width of the finished stripping to allow for loss when diagonally set patchwork is trimmed. For example, on the patchwork in the wallhanging pictured in the colour pages, the finished width of the stripping is 58 cm, so bars needed to be at least 10 cm longer to allow for the angle.

3 Cut four strips of main fabric 68 cm by 8 cm for bars.
Divide strips into two equal lots.
Start sewing right side of wallhanging by sewing two strips together, then one 8-cm bar on right-hand end.

Wallhanging

cut two borders joined through centre

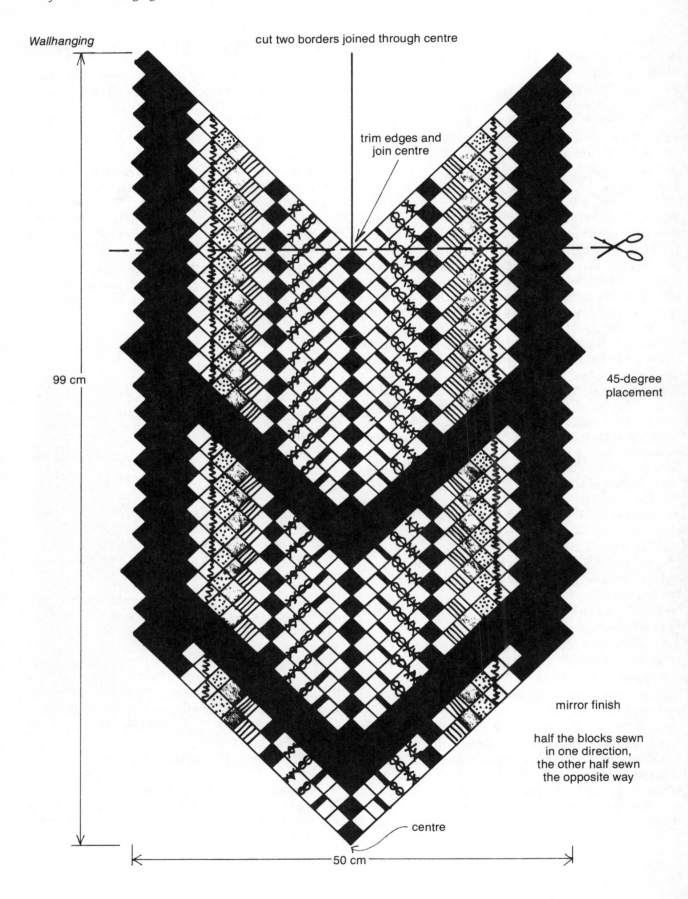

trim edges and
join centre

99 cm

45-degree
placement

mirror finish

half the blocks sewn
in one direction,
the other half sewn
the opposite way

centre

50 cm

4 Next, sew seven strips together, then sew one 8-cm bar making sure that the bar is added to the right-hand end of the set. This now makes a block. Next sew ten strips together for the last set. This will allow you to give your piece a straight edge at the top. Do not cut this yet, however—you need to join the mirror-finished borders first.

5 To finish the right side of the wallhanging, sew the seven-strip block to the two-strip block, sewing a bar to the block of seven. Then sew the set of ten strips to the bar, making sure that all are sewn accurately in line (lay your see-through ruler along the patches to check).
Overlock or zigzag to neaten.

6 Sew the left side of the wallhanging by reversing the procedure of placement and sewing of strips and bars.
Lay your patchwork pieces in place before sewing, making sure you have a mirror finish.
Embellish bars with braid or lace to highlight.
Press the two pieces of completed patchwork.

7 Using a see-through ruler, cut the edges off both sides of the patchwork piecing to straighten.
Place two pieces of patchwork with the lowest point in the centre, with right sides facing in, so that one looks like a mirror image of the other. Make sure that the pattern is equally balanced.
Working on the wrong side, pin then tack, making sure that the seams meet.
Sew a seam through the middle.
Mark across the top of the wallhanging in a straight line, as shown in the illustration on page 58.
Cut off excess fabric.

8 Your patchwork piece should be 94 cm long and 50 cm wide. Cut lining to the same size.
Press patchwork piece and lay face down on top of the lining, with right sides together.
Pin the two layers together on the wrong side then tack, leaving a 20-cm opening on one side.
Straight stitch around all sides.

9 Turn right side out through the opening.
Press, then handstitch to close the opening, using blind stitch.

10 With a 13-mm seam allowance from the top edge of the wallhanging, sew on silk fringe then sew fringe across the bottom of the hanging, 13 mm up from edge.
Straight stitch braid across right on the very edge of the top of the wallhanging, then down one side. Continue until all edges have been finished with braid.

11 To make the four tabs, cut a piece of the main material 60 cm by 14 cm.
Fold fabric lengthwise with right sides facing in. Stitch along raw edges with a 6-mm seam allowance.
Turn right side out so that the seams are centred and the folds are on the outer edges.
Embellish with braid or lace, sewing either side on each edge. Silk fringe and a tassel can also be added to the bottom.
Cut into four equal lengths of 15 cm.
Fold each of these in half and zigzag or overlock the raw edges.
Place and handsew the tabs 13 mm in from the top edge, equal distances apart, on the back of the wallhanging.

Finished wallhanging

Suppliers

Victoria

Arbee Handcrafts
6/20 Lexton Road
Box Hill North Vic. 3129
Tel: (03) 898 9395
(Wholesale only)

Ashburton Bargain Box
289 High Street
Ashburton 3147
Tel: (03) 885 6946

Bead City
373 Camberwell Road
Camberwell 3124
Tel: (03) 882 3382

Boronia Arts and Crafts
247 Dorset Road
Boronia 3155
Tel: (03) 672 1751

Designer Trim
134 Bridge Road
Richmond 3121
Tel: (03) 428 4897
(Wholesale and retail)

Dimmeys
140 Swan Street
Richmond 3121
Tel: 429 5277

155 Maroondah Highway
Ringwood
Tel: 870 6309

80 Nicholson Street
Footscray 3011
Tel: 687 4345

(Also in Dandenong and Geelong)

Dollar Curtains
All stores

E. C. Birch
153 Bridge Road
Richmond 3121
(Wholesale only)

Horizon Fabrics
243 Burwood Road
Hawthorn 3122
Tel: (03) 819 4066

188 York Street
South Melbourne 3205

Lincraft stores in Ballarat, Bendigo, Box Hill, Camberwell, Chadstone, Cheltenham, Croydon, Dandenong, Doncaster, Footscray, Frankston, Geelong, Glen Waverley, Greensborough, Lilydale, Maribyrnong, Melbourne (Australia on Collins, Shop 320, 303 Little Collins Street, Melbourne 3000, tel: 03 650 1609), Mildura, Moe, Moonee Ponds, Preston, Shepparton, Wangaratta, Wantirna South

Patchwork Plus
646 High Street
East Kew 3101
Tel: (03) 859 9356

Remnant Warehouse
1 Edsall Street (at rear)
Malvern 3144
Tel: (03) 500 9397

10–12 Cato Street
Prahran 3181
Tel: (03) 510 1121

Spotlight stores in Bayswater, Bendigo, Bentleigh, Box Hill, Brunswick, Bundoora, Dandenong, Footscray, Frankston, Geelong, Hartwell, Malvern, Mildura, Morwell, Niddrie, Sale, Shepparton, South Yarra, Warrnambool, Werribee

New South Wales

A. A. & Extra Grade Beads
Shop 451
Festival Market Place
Darling Harbour 2000
Tel: 281 8282

The Bead Collection
Shop 114
Old Town Centre
Bankstown 2200
Tel: 708 5045

English Cottage Fabrics
95 Pittwater Road
Boronia Park 2111
Tel: 748 2628

Lincraft stores in Albury, Castle Towers, Charlestown, Dubbo, Grafton, Lismore, Liverpool, Miranda, Orange, Roselands, Sydney (Imperial Arcade, Pitt Street, Sydney 2000, tel: 02 221 5111), Tamworth, Taree, Wagga Wagga

Logan's Fabrics
381 Darling Street
Balmain 2041
Tel: 810 4782

Patches 'N' Pieces
32 Oxford Street
Epping 2121
Tel: 869 8082

Patchwork House
3 Terminus Street
Castle Hill 2154
Tel: 680 3817

Patchwork Plus
Woolworths Arcade
Hurstville 2220
Tel: 580 2486

The Quilting Bee
14 Gordon Village Arcade
Gordon 2072
Tel: 499 2203

Spotlight stores in Albury, Birkenhead Point, Bondi, Campbelltown, Dubbo, Gosford, Liverpool, Merrylands, Newcastle, Penrith, Queanbeyan, Tamworth, Wagga Wagga, Wollongong

Threads 'N' Things
1 Revesby Place
Revesby 2212
Tel: 792 1472

ACT

Bilbo's Crafts
Shop 21, Kippax Fair
Holt 2615
Tel: 254 9370

Lincraft stores in Bellconnen,
Canberra (Shop 803, Canberra Centre,
Anslio Avenue, Civic 2601,
tel: 062 57 4516), Woden

Truly Lois
Cnr Gladstone and Victoria Streets
Hall 2618
Tel: 230 2415

South Australia

Barossa Quilt and Craft Cottage
Angaston–Nuriootpa Main Road
Barossa Valley 5355
Tel: 62 3212

Lincraft stores in Adelaide, (Rundle
Mall Basement, Rundle Mall,
Adelaide 5000, tel: 08 232 4877),
Elizabeth and Tea Tree

Patches and Pieces
Belvidere Road
Saddleworth 5413
Tel: 47 4017

The Quilt Basket
102 Main Street
Yankalilla 5203
Tel: 58 2720

Quilts and Threads
1015 Lower North East Road
Highbury 5089
Tel: 396 3711

Spotlight stores in Adelaide, Christies
Beach, Port Adelaide, Salisbury

Western Australia

Fremantle Crafts and Supplies –
Cottage Crafts
255 South Terrace
South Fremantle 6162
Tel: 336 1525

Gilberts Bridal, Floral & Handcrafts
306 Murray Street
Perth 6000
Tel: 321 9873

Langdale Pty Ltd
33 King Street
Perth 6000
Tel: 322 4188

Lincraft Fabrics
713 Hay Street
Perth 6000
Tel: 09 324 1776

Meg Sheen Craftsman Supplier
308 Hay Street
Subiaco 6008
Tel: 381 8215

The Calico House
2 Napoleon Street
Cottesloe 6011
Tel: 383 3794

The Patchworks of W.A.
394 Fitzgerald Street
North Perth 6006
Tel: 328 9109

The Work Basket
27 Bruce Street
Nedlands 6009
Tel: 386 1065

Queensland

Beads and Beads
Shop 82, Elizabeth Street Level
Queen Street Mall entrance
Myer Centre
Brisbane 4000
Tel: 210 0302

City Remnants
Myer Centre
Brisbane 4000
Tel: 221 6353

Lincraft stores in Brisbane (Shop 237,
Myer Centre, Queen Street, Brisbane
4000, tel: 07 221 0064), Broadbeach,
Loganholme, Rockhampton,
Southport, Toowoomba, Townsville

Patches Etc!
34 Downs Street
North Ipswich 4305
Tel: 812 2011

Patches – Indooroopilly
9 Railway Avenue
Indooroopilly 4068
Tel: 870 3579

Patchwork Supplies
43 Gloucester Street
Highgate Hill 4101
Tel: 844 8381

Spotlight stores in Kedron,
Loganholme, Mt Gravatt, Southport,
Townsville

Tasmania

Colonial Craft Supplies
10 Andrew Street
Brighton 7030
Tel: 68 1445

Denise Craft Connections
46 Binnalong Road
Mornington 7018
Tel: 44 1669

Hobart Craft Supplies
Behind 63 Salamanca Place
Hobart 2000
Tel: 23 8779

Lincraft stores in Burnie, Devonport,
East Hobart, Hobart, Launceston

The Patch Works
91 Patrick Street
Hobart 2000
Tel: 34 2279

Northern Territory

Alice Traders Sewing Centre
2 Schwartz Crescent
Alice Springs 0870
Tel: 52 2450

Tanami Garden Centre
Paterson Street
Tennant Creek
Tel: 62 2809

Weavers Workshop
Parap Shopping Village
Parap Place
Parap 0820
Tel: 81 6986

Yee's Hobbies and Crafts
19a Bishop Street
Stuart Park 0820
Tel: 81 6986

Glossary

backstitch When sewing straight stitch on a machine, pull or push the lever (or whatever your machine has – check instruction booklet) which reverses the stitching. Backstitching ensures that your stitching will not unravel.

bars These are strips of fabric cut to the desired width, usually 5–7.5 cm and the measured length, then preferably embellished before sewing to each set to make a block. Bars can really be lavish and make the border look more interesting and intricate.

blindstitch This is almost invisible and is done by catching a small amount of thread on both pieces of fabric (usually a hem) about every 13 mm.

blocks These are formed when stripping is recut then resewn into sets of five to seven strips. A bar is then added to one side of every set to make a block.

channelling Lines of straight stitching 13 mm apart form channels which can then be threaded with elastic or acrylic macrame cord for trapunto.

embellishing Chosen ribbons, braids and lace can be added along strips in preparation for patchwork to highlight and accentuate colours. You can also embellish bars.

gathering threads Two rows of large stitches about 3 mm apart along the edge to be gathered.

macrame cord This is a soft acrylic cord, preferably of 7-ply thickness and bought by the skein.

overlocking A sewing machine function which cuts off and neatens with close zigzag stitching in one process.

rouleau A thin length of fabric folded in half lengthwise and seamed along the raw edges on wrong side. When turned right side out it is a thin cord which has many uses, such as for ties, button loops and trims. Although rouleau is usually cut on the bias, in this book it is always cut on the straight grain to avoid stitches breaking when the rouleau cords are tied tightly.

sets of stripping These are lengths of stripping ready to use for patchwork. The strips of different materials have been sewn together, then overlocked or zigzagged to neaten.

sets This is stripping which has been embellished, recut, arranged in a patchwork pattern of five to seven pieces, then sewn together and overlocked.

straight stitch This is a normal machine-sewing stitch with about four stitches to the centimetre. Larger straight stitches are used to create gather thread.

stripping Lengths of fabric 2.5–7.5 cm wide cut ready for sewing.

trapunto A traditional Italian embroidery technique which I have adapted for use in bands, cuffs and hems. I sew parallel channels in a length of material and push acrylic macrame thread through with a bodkin. I use this form of trapunto to give body and a glamorous finish to garments.

rouleau hook This is a fine steel hook, 27 cm long, with a latch hook on one end which is used to pull rouleau cords through to the right side after you have sewn the seam on the wrong side.

zigzag This stitch is available on most portable machines and is used to neaten edges after straight stitching is done.

Index